LAST DANCE
IN SHEDIAC

Last Dance *in* Shediac

MEMORIES OF MUM,
MOLLY LAMB BOBAK

Anny Scoones

TouchWood
Editions

TouchWood Editions
www.touchwoodeditions.com

LIBRARY AND ARCHIVES CANADA CATALOGUING IN PUBLICATION
Scoones, Anny, 1957-, author
Last dance in Shediac : memories of mum, Molly Lamb Bobak / Anny Scoones.

Issued in print and electronic formats.
ISBN 978-1-77151-138-4 (paperback).

1. Bobak, Molly Lamb, 1922–2014—Family. 2. Scoones, Anny,1957-.
3. Painters—Canada—Biography. I. Title.

ND249.B554S26 2015   759.11   C2015-904189-9

Editing by Barbara Pulling
Copy editing by Marlyn Horsdal
Cover and interior design by Pete Kohut
Cover image: *Long Beach* by Molly Lamb Bobak
Cover photo: Printed with permission of the author

We gratefully acknowledge the financial support for our publishing activities
from the Government of Canada through the Canada Book Fund and the
Canada Council for the Arts, and from the Province of British Columbia
through the British Columbia Arts Council and the Book Publishing Tax Credit.

15 16 17 18 19   5 4 3 2 1

PRINTED IN CANADA AT FRIESENS

To Heather and Anne, and to the man in the green shirt

CHAPTER ONE

I T WAS FIVE DAYS BEFORE Christmas in 2013, and I was visiting Mum at the Veterans Health Unit in Fredericton. I had flown into town the day before. A vicious ice storm had chased the plane all the way from the bleak, frozen tarmac in Montreal, where I had spent the night at the airport after flying on the red-eye from Victoria.

I had been dreading the experience of sleeping in Montreal's grimy airport, with its musty, grey carpets and flickering fluorescent lights. At one o'clock in the morning I lumbered off the Victoria plane and headed for the Maritime departure gates along an endless, rubber-scented hallway that ran under the runway. Airports always put the waiting areas for Maritime flights in the basement, Mum was fond of pointing out.

I chose a vinyl bench near the window. Outside, the darkness was a blur of blowing snow and the flashing yellow lights of snowplows and salt trucks. Another woman a few seats away was bedding down for the night, and a weary janitor was pushing around a stringy mop that looked dirtier than the floor. Unexpectedly, as I sat there in the silence, I felt a deep contentment float over me, knowing that the next few hours would be a chance to think and doze. I ate a tuna sandwich as I gazed out at the nighttime activity, then organized my bags, made a pillow with my sweater, and stretched out to read a little from the thousand-page novel I was halfway through, about a medieval village and the building of a cathedral.

After a while, I thought I should get ready for bed. My feet ached, so I took off my socks and searched for my foot cream in my bag. When I glanced down at my feet, I got a momentary shock—they looked exactly like Mum's feet, not really foot-shaped but more oval, like bulging little sandbags, with tops that were slightly humped. My lower legs were pale and blotchy, like an English maid's might look after a day of slopping the pigs and cooking the joint—a roast—for dinner. My toenails were thick and yellowish, and I was developing a bunion, which sometimes burned with pain. I credited it to my years and years of wearing tight rubber riding boots, dating as far back as the Fredericton Pony Club where I had first taken riding lessons at the age of ten. I sat massaging my feet with a lovely German herbal ointment at three o'clock in the bowels of the Montreal airport, and then I lay down on the seat and fell fast asleep, a tiny speck protected from the vast white world and the wind blowing furiously on the other side of the glass. By the time I woke up a few hours later, the snow had turned to ice pellets, whipping against the window in the white dawn. The smell of coffee filled the air. Early-morning travellers were arriving, checking their tickets, eating muffins, reading the newspaper, and talking on their cell phones. Two very separate worlds had been divided by only a few hours.

Now Mum was dozing on her bed in the veterans' facility, and I was sitting on a cot covered by a red quilt one of the nurses had found in the storage room down the hall. I had brought three CDs with me: recordings of Elgar's *Enigma Variations* and *Pomp and Circumstance Marches* ("the *Pomp and Circumstance* is so wonderful, so English," Mum always said) and Respighi's *Pines of Rome*, plus an old Rita MacNeil CD featuring the song "Flying on Your Own," one of Mum's favourites. Mum used to hum that song whenever she cleaned our big old house on Lansdowne Street wearing her rubber gloves, though she could never hit the high notes Rita did so well. The nurses had lent us an old CD player from the lounge.

When I'd arrived at noon, Mum was eating lunch with three gentlemen. She had her back to me, but I recognized her fragile head of white hair and her red cashmere sweater, loose around her tiny neck. When I got closer, I could see that she was eating green Jell-O, soothing on her tender throat after a recent operation for a tumour. The surgery had weakened her so much that her thin little hand, bent and misshapen due to years of holding her paintbrush at a certain angle, shook as she brought the Jell-O to her mouth.

Mum's hand reminded me of the feet of my old canary, Pip, back home in Victoria. We kept him in a beautiful cage that hung in the dining room window, so that he would receive the morning sun. He was a joyful bird who had already lived far beyond his expected years. His twisted, pink feet were no longer able to grasp his perch, so I had devised a series of flat steps for him to climb. Pip had been through many of life's ups and downs with me—tumultuous relationships, difficult domestic moves, election wins and defeats as a municipal councillor, and even KGB problems in Belarus. Now he was an ancient fellow with contorted feet, and every day when I woke up, I would call, "Morning, Pip!" anxious to hear his peep and chirp in return. One of these days, I knew, I would find him lying peacefully dead among the marigolds I picked for him every day from the garden. On that sad day, I would bury him in the back garden with Miss Kitty, a strange old stray we'd brought to town with us from the farm. On Mum's visits out west, Miss Kitty had always put wine corks in her shoes during the night.

Poor little Pip with his feet, and poor Mum with her hands. However, we had had a grand reunion back in her room—she always kept vermouth in her cupboard, along with two beautiful antique Italian wineglasses, so we wasted no time in celebrating my arrival, and then she didn't seem so fragile after all.

PINES OF ROME is a frustrating piece of music to play in a veterans' care facility, because it's so soft in some sections and so loud in others. When it was soft, Mum said she couldn't hear it, and when I turned it up, it blasted the music down the hall and a man named Orville yelled at us to turn down the "noise." Mum and I both loved the Elgar. The first time I heard it, I was driving in the rain down a misty highway near Victoria. The attack on the World Trade Center in New York had happened a few days earlier, and everyone was still shocked by that event, including the stories about the poor people who had tried to jump to safety. When Elgar's *Variations* came on the radio, it made me weep with its tenderness—I had to drive off onto a side road and wipe my eyes. A painting has never caused me to have that reaction, but when I asked Mum later if she had ever seen a picture that made her weep, she said immediately, "Yes, Cezanne's apples, when I first saw them. Oh, the passion in those apples. It changed my life."

Mum and I both loved to hear Rita MacNeil's Nova Scotia voice bellowing out her songs, but that evening, after the "Working Man" song about the miners, Mum said, "That's enough," and then, after a pause, she added, "Do you know what dear Rita said before she died? She said, 'Put my ashes in a teapot, two if necessary.' What a good soul."

Mum's window looked out over busy Regent Street, which was covered in fresh snow. Across the street was a little mall where I had ventured that afternoon, mainly to get some air after the hot staleness of Mum's room and the stuffy, hospital-kitchen smells of canned soup and mashed potatoes with gravy. I bought the *Globe and Mail* at a cramped Indian convenience store that smelled of curry and spices and sold fresh samosas in bags on the counter. The streets were deserted. The only light came from the red Scotiabank sign on the frozen brick wall at the end of the mall and a few barren tree branches twinkling with white lights. A solitary, black figure trudged along the unplowed sidewalk.

Fredericton was recovering from the wild winter storm that had followed me from Quebec. On the television in the hallway, after our dinner of pork cutlets with orange sauce, pea soup, and vanilla pudding, we had watched the strong, controlled Ontario premier, Kathleen Wynne, advising people to remain calm, to help their elderly neighbours, and to stay indoors while the Hydro crews repaired the broken wires. Two Toronto hospitals had lost power and were on generators, and pasty-looking mayor Rob Ford asked people to be patient, even though they might not have power again until Christmas Day.

The windows in Mum's room opened, which I thought was very civilized. My cot was beside the window, so I could reach over periodically and turn the handle, letting the freezing air blow straight into my face. That was not only refreshing, but also a kind of rebirth, a start-over moment, when reality seemed to have become too much. Not that the situation was in any way bad, but it was *different*, an adjustment from the not-so-long-ago times when Mum would walk to the market from her house on Kensington Court on Saturdays to buy pork liver for the dogs, or a cow tongue, which she would boil and then serve cold in sandwiches. Until recently, on clear winter nights, she'd skied under the moon through the woods along the frozen river.

Mum used to say about death, "When it's time, just put me on an ice floe like an old Eskimo, and let me drift away," and then we would make a joke about what would happen when she went through the Reversing Falls downriver at Saint John. But now, she said she rarely thought about death. Perhaps the closer we travel toward our end, the less we think about it. I had always felt at ease talking to Mum about death: not just her death, but death in general. I thought about it far more than she did, perhaps because when I had the farm in North Saanich, I saw so much death—piglets crushed by their mother's bulk, eagles grabbing helpless chickens, weary horses who had come to the end of their days, baby birds who tumbled out of nests in the barn rafters and hit the cold cement below. I had almost died myself once on the farm. I was stung on the neck by a bee under the pear tree, and I fell into a blissful, pain-free state in which my mind felt separate from my body and I seemed to be drifting into infinity. I was rudely brought back to earth by a nervous, perspiring, young paramedic on my kitchen floor. I remember that I didn't really want to come back from that lovely, calm state, whatever it was. I was really torn about whether to return.

Maybe death was not so sad, not such a bad thing, not to be feared at all, I thought as I lay on my cot in Mum's room. Maybe it was a celebration of life, a quiet ending to the phase we call "being alive," and

I couldn't help wondering where I would have gone had the paramedic not brought me back. The possibility of peaceful pleasure had seemed so within my reach. Maybe our whole idea is wrong. Maybe death is an entrance into something lovely. People say humans came from the sea, but maybe before that we came from space, to which we will return, floating.

My family—Mum, Dad, my older brother, and I—moved to Fredericton when I was five years old, from England, where Mum and Dad had spent time painting, teaching, and travelling around Europe. We arrived on a cold winter's day, pulling up in front of a brownstone house with a blue door on Lansdowne Street. The snowbanks were higher than my head. We stayed in that neighbourhood throughout my childhood, living in several different houses. Although it flooded when the Saint John River rose every spring, it was quiet, tree-lined, and pretty, close to town and to the university where Dad was the artist in residence.

In the warmer seasons, we'd go for drives in the New Brunswick countryside, where crumbling, abandoned farmhouses sat among gnarly, old orchards in a tangle of wildflower meadows. Mum and Dad would pick wild apples and chokecherries and bring them home, where the fruit would cook for days on the stove until it boiled down to a beautiful, thick, rose-coloured jelly. Dad would bottle it in glass jars and wrap them in purple, plastic, pantyhose packages tied with raffia to give away as Christmas presents. Dad's brother, Ernie, had been a pantyhose salesman in Hamilton, and we had somehow ended up with boxes and boxes of petite-sized pantyhose. Mum and Dad would take time out on our country trips to sketch on the banks of clear streams while I paddled in the reeds with my collection of troll dolls. Sometimes Mum would wander farther afield to forage. One time she found a huge cranberry patch in a dusty ditch.

And now, at the Veterans Health Unit, Mum was eating baby food—pea soup and butterscotch pudding, and commercial jam in plastic packets. It was a good thing she wasn't senile, because we had a laugh at how we really do become babies again eventually: back to babies, but this time with a lifetime of knowledge and memories—smart babies. Even the noises we make in the night when we're old sound similar to those of a happy, gurgling baby. Mum told me she had had a dream one night about swimming in Deer Lake with her friend Cedric when they were little. Deer Lake is in Burnaby, British Columbia, where Mum spent her childhood, and Cedric lived next door. In the dream, Mum explained, it was autumn, and damp. "A long dirt driveway led up to our house, with meadows on either side, and along it was an apple tree, bare except for one red apple still clinging onto the branch, wet from the rain. Funny what one remembers."

A NURSE CAME in every night around nine to give Mum her eye drops. Sometimes the nurses sat on the end of her bed to chat. It was such a comfort, and those dear nurses, Kay, Ashley, Amanda, Gail, Claire, and Kathy, or Mo, the social worker, were never in a hurry and would bring tea if we asked. One nurse even sewed a button onto Mum's sweater one late evening. Mum's bed had sides so she wouldn't fall out, like an adult crib, but I took them off while I was there. Her bed also had a plastic sheet under the flannelette one. There was nothing I could do about that; my cot had a plastic sheet too. Mum said she was glad that's a problem *we* didn't have; we had bad ears and terrible nerves, but good bladders. Mum was the only resident who didn't wear a bib at meal times. "I just discreetly placed it on my lap," she confided, "to not hurt the staff's feelings. Watching someone change is almost worse than going through it yourself."

Sometimes I took Mum for a walk along the hall for exercise. She could only shuffle, because her legs were still so weak following her throat operation. The building was designed in a square, so we'd "walk around the block," sometimes pausing in the small lounge to watch the CBC news or the weather channel. According to the television, it was mild and sunny at home in Victoria. In the big lounge near the dining room there were numerous recliners and a Christmas tree. Sometimes we sat in the recliners for a minute on our strolls, "just for a change, and to rest," Mum said. I couldn't help but remember the long walks she'd take along the university trails in the autumn in Fredericton, the woods ablaze in reds and ochres and rusty oranges, and her jaunts along the wild, grassy banks of the river and past the soccer field on the Green, an area used for local sporting events. Mum had painted many a soccer game down there, just a block from our house, and Dad used to launch his aluminum boat off the yellow, sandy beach and catch bass as he drifted downriver under the aging, green Princess Margaret Bridge.

The Christmas tree in the big lounge was covered in decorations, each bearing a tag labelled with the name of a veterans' home resident. Mum asked, "Is mine there?" so I searched through the branches. There was a silver globe for Ora—he'd fought in the Korean War, and his room was next to Mum's—a train engine for Pearly, and an ornament for a man Mum loved, whom they all called "the Mayor." The Mayor rarely left his room because he was so sad over the death of his wife. Finally I found Mum's decoration, a beautiful golden pear. Mum said, "Take it," and I thought that was a grand idea, to take it home, all the way back to Victoria, and put it on our own tree, and then I would think of Mum every Christmas.

We resumed our walk, passing through the kitchen area where women in blue hairnets and rubber gloves were preparing lunch, setting out the bibs on the tables, and putting plastic cups of juice at each place. We continued down the north hallway. "Am I really in a home?" Mum asked as we moved slowly along on the polished linoleum, Mum in the Cowichan slippers I had brought her from home. "It's so surreal," she said. "It was my choice to come here, of course. I didn't want a girl at the house after Bruno died. It was such an intrusion, and they're good to me here."

When I'd first brought Mum up to see the veterans' place, on a freezing January afternoon, she'd said, "Anny, one thing about me is that I'm positive," which, of course, meant she planned to make the most of her stay and to try not to fade away into a depression. Mum was never really the depressive type anyway, though Dad and I were. We reflected a lot, and Mum had all this energy that couldn't wait for us as we sat morosely staring into space. I'd thought at first that the Veterans

Health Unit was a strange choice for Mum to make, somewhere so devoid of the life she'd known, but I remembered hearing her say once about the last house she and Dad lived in, on Kensington Court, "This is Bruno's house, done with his taste. Don't get me wrong, I love it, it's comfortable, but I would never have those fake-leather couches. Bruno knew the furniture salesman and traded a painting of a fishing camp for them—one of his pink sunset scenes."

The Kensington Court house was full of art. Soup was always simmering on the stove, and Dad's spindly, red geraniums hung in the large windows that overlooked his lush garden, packed with peas climbing up strings and voluptuous tomatoes he had bred and named "Bruno's Best." Neighbours constantly dropped in and sat themselves down among the stacks of books and pottery bowls full of fruit on Dad's handmade tile tables.

Dad set out dishes of dog cookies for friends who dropped in with their pets. Heather and Anne, whom Mum and Dad referred to as "the girls from next door," although they were both lawyers, would stop by after work with their dogs, Arthur and Sophie. Sophie was a spaniel rescued from a puppy mill in Nova Scotia. She had no teeth, so her pink tongue hung sideways from her mouth. She'd doze on Mum's lap while everyone had a glass of wine.

Dad served their guests nuts and chips he bought at a discount store called Giant Tiger. Mum would mutter under her breath as she cut up a few celery sticks, "Bruno's a millionaire, and he still shops at that foul Giant Tiger—I refuse to go there." When Dad heard her, he'd get a familiar exasperated smirk on his face. Mum and Dad had a manic friend who visited occasionally and talked non-stop while munching on Dad's snacks. One time she ate all the dog cookies by mistake instead and didn't even notice.

Mum told me once that she was not as strong as Gran (her mother) or me. She was a "capitulator," she said. I wondered if maybe a capitulator wasn't the stronger person, to relent and then continue on. I don't know how a person can do that. Maybe that's why Mum called me "Big Anny," and always said, "You're so strong; you don't need defending." She was half-joking; I wasn't big by any means, but since Mum had been in the veterans' facility, sometimes I felt massive due to the frailty around me.

I had always assumed that neither of my parents would end up in an "old folks' home." At a stretch, Dad would have seemed more the Veterans Health Unit type—his roots were humble, and he found solace in the company of ordinary people. He had seen the horrors of war when he worked overseas as a war artist, and having been a poor, Polish immigrant, he understood about life's struggles. And yet here was Mum, ensconced in a world of pad-covered recliner chairs, Legion singalongs, ball-tossing exercises done sitting down, plastic cups of juice, Jell-O, and fluorescent lights. "Mum, this really isn't a home. It's more like a hotel for old people," I'd tell her, and that softened the blow for both of us, temporarily.

An amusing activity Mum and I embarked on, alone in her room, was list making. One afternoon I suggested she list off her favourite people in the world, without thinking about it, just spontaneously. She shouted out Bora Laskin's name immediately, and then Henry Morgentaler, Tommy Douglas, Dolly Parton, Rachel Carson, and Kermit the Frog. I added Charles Darwin as my choice. Bora Laskin was a forward-thinking Canadian lawyer and judge, compassionate in his role as Chief Justice of the Supreme Court. He was one of the first to decide in favour of the right to spousal support after divorce.

"What a combination!" Mum said as we laughed over our list. The poet Stevie Smith earned an honourable mention, mainly due to her poem "Not Waving but Drowning." Finally we added Elizabeth May—"What a brave woman she is," Mum said—and then Bill Clinton (Mum's choice). She sat up in bed and imitated Bill, waving her finger and saying in a southern accent, "I did not have sexual relations with that woman..."

One afternoon the Legion held a Christmas party, and there was a Santa Claus who handed out chocolates from a walker. Mum and I each had a shortbread and then took to the hallway for exercise. The last time I'd come for a visit, in November, the veterans' unit bus had taken us to the cenotaph on Remembrance Day. I had to persuade Mum to come, but it was a good outing—the bus was warm, and the nurses gave us blankets for our legs.

The Fredericton cenotaph is down the hill beside the massive stone cathedral with its slender steeple and green copper roof. The amber Saint John River flows alongside the Green, which is dotted with statues, fountains, historical plaques, flower beds, and benches. In summer the banks of the river are covered in reeds and wildflowers: daisies, buttercups, Queen Anne's lace. There are sandy coves where you almost expect to see Mole and the other characters from *The Wind in the Willows*. One summer Mum petitioned Mayor Woodside, who operated a riverboat cruise business, for the city to stop spraying pesticides along the riverbanks, and he took heed. Mum loyally voted for him ever afterwards.

The veterans' unit bus parked right next to the ceremonial area, and we watched the Remembrance Day parade before observing the usual two minutes of silence. It was a bitter day, with dead, brown leaves frozen onto the frosty grass under a steel-grey sky. The Mounties marched by first in their red coats, then the armed forces veterans in their blue blazers and medals, then the Legion ladies in their white skirts, carrying big purple-and-gold-embossed flags. Cadets brought up the rear, marching all out of step in their big, black boots and ill-fitting pants. The boy who played "The Last Post" was a chubby teenager in a tight, red jacket who missed only one note.

Although Mum and Dad had both enlisted when the Second World War broke out and gone through basic training, they didn't fight because they were sent overseas as official Canadian war artists. To become a war artist, you had to enter a competition. Dad won first prize, and Mum came second. Dad painted scenes from the field, and the war painting of his that I remember best, which I saw in a catalogue, showed a dental truck on a war-torn field. A soldier was lying in the back of the van, having his tooth pulled. Mum claimed Dad made that scene up, but it didn't matter: the subject was unforgettable, and, in a strange way, also comical—a soldier surrounded by the violence and horror of war undergoing something so ordinary. Mum stayed in England much of the time and painted life in the barracks.

After the Remembrance Day ceremony, the marchers proceeded down Queen Street, past the gleaming art gallery, the great stone legislature, the downtown shops, and the handsome, old, red-brick buildings. Crowds of spectators stood frozen on the curb, wrapped in scarves and winter coats. Our bus had joined the procession at the end, so we were in the parade too. People along the route began to wave and clap for the old veterans on the bus; one woman held up a poster she'd made that said THANK YOU. The chief of police, a woman named Leanne Fitch, dressed in a crisp, white shirt with regalia on the shoulders, saluted as the bus slowly passed by.

Mum started waving back, and we wept a bit. We were both a little emotional. We always cried when Kermit the Frog sang "The Rainbow Connection"—he was such a gentle dear. Mum even claimed that Kermit was her favourite American. So we were wet-eyed on the bus, at the respect people showed but also at the horror of war, the idea of defending our country together, our great, kind Canada, and the eternal struggle of good against evil. Then the bus turned up Regent Street and took us back to the veterans' unit, where we had some tea to warm up. Mum had dubbed her new abode "The Barracks," and she referred to her bed as "the fart sack." "That's what we called it in the war," she explained.

The freezing rain and ice pellets turned to slush a few days into my December visit, and the snowbanks on the corners were coated in a brown film. Staying at the veterans' home was okay—my cot was comfy, and the peace and quiet were calming. Every day I ventured out somewhere for a walk. One afternoon I bundled up and walked down the street to the Irving gas station, circled past the CBC studios, then trundled through waist-high snow back to the veterans' parking lot. A better walk, I discovered, was around the perimeter of the hospital, which was plowed. Although the wind and icy rain stung my face, the cold air soothed my mind. The hospital was a massive, white steel building trimmed with bright-yellow tubing, reported to have the best gift shop in Fredericton. Everything they sold was made in Canada, from woollen toques to local soaps to fudge. Maritimers love fudge. It's for sale everywhere, along with dish cloths knitted from soft, thick fabric strips.

As I rounded the snowdrifts at the edge of the building, I thought of Dad a year earlier, staying on the fourth floor of the hospital and dealing so well with his throat cancer. He had to be fed through a tube inserted into his stomach, and he breathed and spoke through a tube in his throat, but he still managed to make a joke in the hospital lobby when I was taking him home for the afternoon. He had to use a wheelchair at that point, and there were many wheelchairs in the lobby to choose from. Dad pointed to one with a particularly wide seat and said, holding the tube in his neck steady and labouring over his words, "That one's for a woman." Dad was no feminist, and he always thought it was fun to buck the trend of feminism. Really, he did it to be irritating.

As I walked back along the salted cement walkway toward the Veterans Health Unit, I remembered a clever painting Mum had done in that very spot. It showed three patients sitting in wheelchairs with IV bags attached; they were out in the bitter cold in the dead of winter, smoking. One was wearing fuzzy pink slippers and another a ragged-looking dressing gown, and they all had bony hands and pale, drawn faces. Mum called the painting *Life and Death*.

I left Mum's place on Christmas Eve afternoon. Her friend Heather drove me to the Fredericton airport, and Mum felt strong enough to come along in Heather's warm Volvo, which was encrusted with ice and salt. It was a dull day, the sun trying to pierce the white winter sky above black branches. The ice storm had passed and was now hitting Newfoundland. The power was still out in Toronto, but the planes were back on schedule.

Heather drove steadily over the thick patches of ice covering Lincoln Road. Lincoln is a suburb of Fredericton, a stretch of road along the river with a few gas stations and prefab houses. I noticed that the Dari Delite was still there, a pink shack by the side of the road adorned with pictures of sundaes with cherries on top. I had a banana split there forty years ago with a high school friend who lived nearby. The motel looked sad in the cold, with only one car in its parking lot. There used to be a pizza place on the site, and when Uncle Ernie, Dad's brother, came to stay with us, he'd take me there for pizza, just the two of us.

After Uncle Ernie married a woman named Elma, whom he'd met at an Arthur Murray dance lesson, we never went for pizza again, because Elma took control of his diet. "No more pizza for you, Ernie," she'd order without looking up from her crocheting. "You'll get fat." Uncle Ernie would sigh, but when he went fishing with Dad on the Miramichi River, they'd take coolers of beer and bologna sandwiches with them and stock up on Cheezies, Bugles, and salted nuts along the way. Poor Mum was left at home to entertain Elma, who, in addition to crocheting, was interested mostly in watching television, drinking tea, and eating cookies.

"What a lovely day," Mum said as Heather drove us past the Irving gas station. "The light is gentle on the old eyes." Mum and Dad and I used to laugh about the Irving stations. They were called Big Stops, and that struck us as humorous. The Big Stops usually had gift shops as well as fast food—salt and pepper shakers shaped like lobsters, spoons with the provincial flower on the handle. Elma loved to collect spoons, and she told us she had a huge collection from all over Canada.

Heather pulled up to the icy curb at the airport, and I hugged Mum goodbye. I used to get weepy when I said goodbye to her, but now it was different, perhaps because I had established a good life and a home I loved in Victoria. I finally felt I had a purpose, after years of feeling quite useless. Mum was sad that I was leaving, just as I'd been sad as a child when she left on her European trips every winter—I'd be crying as she and Dad went off gaily to paint Spanish villages and crowded Barcelona beaches. Now I was heading home to resume the life I had built for myself. We had reversed roles.

The Fredericton airport was quiet. I lugged my bags through security but was stopped because of two old-fashioned drinking glasses Mum had given me. The staff on duty eventually let me through. Had they really thought I was going to hit the pilot over the head with drinking glasses? Fredericton airport has the strictest security I have ever experienced; one time they took a jar of Dad's apple jelly from me, and another time they confiscated a bologna the size of a missile. It did look like a bomb—it had been on sale at Fredericton's Victory Meat Market, and Dad made me buy the whole thing to save money. Sometimes he'd drive us crazy with his obsession about saving money, even though we knew it came from his terrible childhood experiences. He and Ernie had actually had to live under a bridge in Toronto and eat scraps from restaurant trash at one point. A publisher once brought out a book about Dad, and in it was the saddest photograph I had ever seen: his family, new to Canada, forlorn and looking like small, shocked ghosts.

Soon I was up above the clouds, with some tomato juice and a foil packet of pretzels on my tray. I love flying into the night. The route from Fredericton to Toronto is often over Montreal, which is magical: a mass of twinkling, amber neighbourhoods, busy urban streets, and bridges over the black swaths of river. Gradually the brightness becomes sparse, and it's pitch black again. Flying to Victoria from Toronto is equally wonderful—the vastness of the country, the emptiness below. I find it truly moving to see all the little communities across our huge country. Although we have our problems—the terrible legacy of our residential schools, the tar sands, plump, pink-faced Mike Duffy (Mum called him "Puffy"), and last year the shootings in Ottawa—it's still a great country. I was young and obsessed with my trolls and my old horse when Pierre Trudeau was prime minister, but I remember seeing him on television and hearing him say the words "this great, great country," which for some reason have remained firmly in my memory. I feel those simple words have influenced many of my adult views and decisions. Mum had met many of Canada's leaders when they came to our house to buy art. In later years, she loved Jack Layton, and she always said that Stephen Harper's lips were too shiny for a prime minister.

A few years earlier, on one of my trips to Fredericton, I had been asked to make a speech at a gathering at the Beaverbrook Hotel. The gathering was held in Mum's honour, to celebrate her art and her life. Hundreds turned out, finely dressed, sipping white wine in the ballroom with its massive glass chandeliers and round tables covered in thick white linen. The host was a local CBC Radio personality. It was a grand event. I spoke about the travels Mum and I had taken together, and the thoughts we'd shared on our walks, and I named a few of the men who made Mum swoon: Mr. Darcy from *Pride and Prejudice* (especially in the person of Colin Firth, the British actor); Prince Andrei from the Russian film version of *War and Peace*; Pinchas Zukerman, the violinist and conductor; the handsome opera singer Mum kept calling "Placebo Flamingo"; and Kermit the Frog. I quickly added, "Dad is not on this list—he's on another list," which made the audience roar with laughter. I glanced down at Dad at our table, and he was smirking like Archie Bunker, wearing a disdainful but resigned look.

After the elegant dinner of steak and salad, Mum and I got back up on the stage to say good night. She was frail but so pleased to be honoured, and as I guided her back down the three steps off the stage, she raised her arms above her head, as if cheering for a sports team, and yelled, "I LOVE CANADA!"

It was a happy night. Mum and I decided to walk home, and we ambled arm in arm past darkened houses and the stone cathedral with its distinctive spire, then under the old railway bridge. A car pulled up beside us. It was Dad and his friends. "Do you girls need a ride?" he asked. Without missing a beat or even looking up, Mum said, "You couldn't afford us." We convulsed in hysterics. "Try the other side of the river," I added as we waved them away.

In Victoria, I stepped off the propeller plane onto the wet, black tarmac at midnight on Christmas Eve. With the time change, Mum would be fast asleep now in her hot little room under her Hudson's Bay blanket, with good memories of my visit until next time. She'd promised to do a few leg exercises and keep up her walks in the hall to become strong again. But somehow, I suspected that, instead of shuffling around the Barracks, she might prefer to listen to her beloved CBC, *Ideas in the Afternoon* or *The Next Chapter*, while lying comfortably in her "fart sack."

CHAPTER TWO

THE AIR ON THE PACIFIC coast felt soft and damp, with whiffs of cedar and salt in the gentle sea breeze. A few years earlier, the Victoria airport had erected a marvellous sculpture of towering, colourful flowers, bent to look as if they were blowing in the wind. They made my heart leap every time I returned.

My friend Mikki and our dog, Archie, were at the airport to meet me. Archie is the newest member of our family, a not-so-bright but lovable hound mix rescued, apparently, from a roadside in Alabama. He came to us with the name Banjo, but Archie suits him better. Archie is not permitted inside the airport, so he always waits patiently on his towel in the back seat of the car.

Mikki and Archie and I—along with Pip, the old canary, and our cats, Jimmy, Baby Girl, and Sophie—live in a quirky area of Victoria called James Bay, one of the oldest parts of town. Emily Carr's birthplace, an elegant Victorian house surrounded by roses, lilies, primroses, and English shrubs, is just up the street. The Legislative Buildings, on the Inner Harbour, are lit up nightly, making the grounds look like a fairyland. People knit sweaters for telephone poles in our neighbour-hood, and hang teacups in trees and plant cabbages on the boulevards.

Christmas week was quiet in James Bay. The days were grey, with low cloud hanging over the bare hawthorns on our street, and the sea almost the same colour as the sky. We visited my two old horses, who were boarded on a farm out by the hospital; before I left for Fredericton, I'd hung cheap red dollar-store stockings on their stall doors and filled them with carrots. Winter in Victoria is hard on livestock—there's a lot of mud, and the ongoing dampness isn't good for their skin.

On Boxing Day Archie and I set out on our nightly stroll. It was a dark night with no moon, but strings of coloured lights illuminated the rhododendrons being tossed by the wind. Some neighbours had hung Christmas balls in the hawthorns and cherry trees on the boulevard. There was a light rain, but the air was fresh as we walked briskly along Dallas Road by the ocean.

There's a pond on the route, man-made, among a grove of cottonwoods, willows, and maples. In the spring it is full of duck families, but that evening I noticed a huddle of people at one end. As we walked closer, I caught the faint aromas of hot chocolate and apple cider, and in the water was a parade of model boats, remote-controlled by a group of old men on the far edge of the pond. Each boat was strung with tiny coloured lights; some had their sails sparkling, others their funnels, and they were doing figure eights in a perfect, silent procession.

Archie and I stood on the sidewalk and watched. It was so quaint, much more amusing than watching real boats sail past in the Inner Harbour. There was something very special and endearing about seeing those little boats on that drizzly, dark Boxing Day eve on Dallas Road, with the captains silently huddled together under the maple trees while their supportive wives sipped hot cider nearby.

Archie and I venture out to the Dallas Road sea walk and beach every morning before dawn. Sometimes our path is lit by a glowing moon, far out and high above the sea. Across the strait is a line of lights at Port Angeles, a town beneath the Olympic Mountains, which are always capped in snow. The barges and freighters anchored in the strait, their sterns alight as they bob in the waves, wait patiently for the yellow pilot boat with the red light on its bow to guide them out to the great ocean beyond.

Whenever I see the tankers, I remember the time I had scarlet fever. I was twenty years old, living in Vancouver, and had fallen deathly ill with this horrid disease. Mum came out from Fredericton to nurse me back to health, although it took a good few weeks. I lay in bed, semi-aware of the world, while Mum sat at my little kitchen table looking out at English Bay, painting delicate watercolours of the yellow freesias that my employers at the theatre company had sent. From time to time, she would put cold face cloths on my forehead. She always told the story, years later, of how when she'd asked me, "Where does it hurt?" I'd answered in a semi-conscious state with a little moan, "At the opera." I can still remember how the faint odour of Mum's cigarette smoke blended with the beautiful fragrance of the freesias and the soft breeze that wafted through the airy apartment. When I was finally well enough to sit up and have a bit of soup (which Mum made from a bone she bought from a butcher on Davie Street), Mum chuckled, "The tankers are in the harbour today showing their red bottoms." That meant the ships were empty and waiting to be loaded at the docks. To this day, when I spot tankers I always look to see if their red bottoms are exposed.

The sunrise on Dallas Road is different every day, but it always gives me an immense inner joy, or awe. I know it's a cliché, but I get a calm and contented feeling knowing that the sun will come up again tomorrow. I stroll along in the dark, listening to the waves wash onto the shore below, and I feel a deep satisfaction, as if I am truly part of nature. I believe this feeling came from an experience I had in Belarus in 1996.

I was on my way to deliver a load of cargo to the Minsk orphanage. Victoria residents who had heard about my "mission" had donated a vast collection of snowsuits, toiletries, toys, and school supplies. It was January in Belarus—bleak and dark. I have always had a fascination with the Eastern Bloc and Russia, and empathy for the people, so there I was, in the freezing Minsk airport, trying to bribe my way past the pale, young guards with Rogers' chocolates and some cash. I didn't quite make it; a moustachioed general in a thick grey coat, carrying a big gun, took me into a bunker and questioned me for hours about the cargo for the orphans. Who was my black-market contact? he demanded over and over, despite my assurances there wasn't one. In the end, I was confined for ten days in a tiny room with bars on the windows and a filthy toilet with no seat. A man brought me food every day—vodka, bologna, jars of pickled vegetables, and once a piece of black bread. I was interrogated endlessly, but I had no answers except the truth, which the KGB questioners didn't believe: I had organized the trip on my own—I was not a spy!

How had this experience made me feel part of nature? Well, under so much interrogation, I began to lose my usual way of thinking. That brought me closer to something we all have inside ourselves, something deeper, that is more akin to a flower, or to a stone, or to a butterfly, or even a mosquito. The realization hit me that we are all the same, composed of the same matter, all part of the same world.

So when I was released and I returned to the North Saanich farm where I was living, I was of a slightly different mindset. One warm spring day I was lying on the lawn when I noticed a tiny purple violet about to open its flower. A warm feeling ran through me. I felt part of the brave little violet, part of nature, and the feeling has stayed with me to this day. It's like a secret I carry around inside. It's not as if I talk to plants or stones or kelp. It's simply the knowledge that I am no more important than they are, and perhaps less.

Mum sometimes said she envied the deep contentment I had come to know. She understood that we are part of nature, but she didn't really *feel* it herself. Possibly that was why, on a certain level, she and I never completely saw eye to eye. Perhaps, too, that was why her paintings were so vivid, so vibrant, so full of life: because she saw the life force in the world and it drove her to paint it. But she painted as an observer and a lover of life, which is different from feeling part of it. Perhaps if she'd felt *part* of nature, her paintings might have been less yearning and more compassionate, more empathetic. There's a sliver of difference between a wonderful painting and a wonderful painting that moves you deeply. I heard Mum say once that she'd never become a great artist or be as daring as someone like Picasso because she didn't have the courage. I thought that was a very honest thing to admit.

Sometimes, when the dawn light on Dallas Road is just right after a clear night, the distant islands seem to be hovering in the glow above the water. The illusion lasts for only a moment. As light gradually fills the meadows and hedgerows above the weathered bluffs, the day's life appears. In the spring, there's a luminescent hummingbird who sits among the burnt-orange rosehips and blackberry bushes. Oystercatchers swoop from rock to rock, shrieking in delight as the tide recedes and they pick tender morsels from the rock crevices with their long red beaks. In the winter, there is a family of harlequin ducks, with their rust chests and beautiful markings, streaks of white and dark green. Rotund buffleheads with their puffy heads of downy white feathers bob in the surf alongside the gulls.

The beaches along Dallas Road are divided from one another by pink-and-grey slabs of rock, engraved by prehistoric glacier activity. Kelp washes up on the pebbled, black shore and gets caught in the weather-beaten driftwood. Oddly shaped milky-white and purple shells, translucent amber agates, emerald-green sea anemones, and pieces of frosted, salt-washed glass glint like jewels in the tidal pools, even on a cloudy day. It is not completely peaceful among the meadows, trees, hedgerows, and beaches of Dallas Road. Not so long ago there was a random stabbing—at midnight, but still, the word "random" made it all the more frightening—at the shelter out on the point. A few harmless, homeless people often slept in the old green hut; Archie and I passed it every morning on our walks, and there were usually beer cans and cigarette butts strewn on the cement below the benches. Still, hearing about that stabbing made me more cautious, and I was always relieved when a jogger passed us in the dark.

I had never been nervous about being attacked or mugged, and neither had Mum. We seemed to have a streetwise protective aura about us, or maybe we'd just been lucky. My sense of ease, I think, came from working at the Wilmot Downs racetrack in Fredericton from an early age, when I stabled my horse, Missy, there in a ramshackle barn. The barn also housed numerous weathered relics, racetrack men who were usually peacefully drunk on whisky. I always felt safe with them, and I was. My job was collecting urine from the winning horse on race nights for drug testing. I was handed a cup on the end of a long stick, and as the steaming, sinewy horse was hosed off, I had to hold the cup strategically and whistle. Those were happy days, my coming-of-age years at the old racetrack, on late nights that smelled of French fries and horse liniment. That was where I became wise to the world.

Mum was a bit of a tomboy herself when she was young, and she'd told me stories about how much she loved hanging around the Vancouver dockyards. There's something romantic about racetracks and dockyards at night—steam and dust, dampness and fading light, working men bustling around, too busy to pay attention to kids who aren't pretty little girls. Mum was very independent as a young woman too. Once, when she was in the army, she was hitchhiking in Ontario and was picked up by a nice fellow in a truck. They were driving along silently in the night when he mentioned that he had to make a quick detour to check on his cabin in the woods. Mum thought it would be delightful to see his cabin, so on they went, down numerous dirt lanes into the deep forest, until they came to an abandoned shack. Mum suddenly became aware of the situation and said sternly that she'd better be going, because the army would be out searching for her. The man turned white with fear and drove her straight to Kingston, where she was stationed.

I thought of Mum in the mornings as the sun gently rose in the east, over Clover Point, creating a slit of pale rose-gold under the opal mists floating above the dark sea. She would be having her tea and scrambled eggs with Ora and Pearly, and then her eye drops, listening to Rita MacNeil on her tape deck, or maybe some Christmas music.

CHAPTER THREE

I LIVED FOR MANY YEARS ON a farm close to the Victoria airport, and every year at Christmastime I'd think about Merlin, a smelly, old goat with stunted legs and a pungent beard whom I had rescued from Salt Spring Island and taken to live with me. Merlin would have terrible coughing fits that sounded a lot like Dad in the bathroom in the mornings. When Mum came out west to visit, Merlin sometimes accompanied us on our walks, and when he had a coughing attack, we'd have to stop and wait for him to recover before proceeding farther along the trail.

One morning Mum and I walked on ahead of Merlin, and when we arrived back at the log house on the farm, he was nowhere to be found. We feared he had either had a heart attack in the tall grass or fallen down an old well. We fretted all day and retraced our steps, but to no avail. Then, just as dusk was falling, Merlin came trotting as fast as his legs would take him down the driveway, bleating in a furious panic, and headed straight past us toward the house. He always slept on the porch, with Alice-Mary, my portly black Labrador, in her basket. Mum and I went into gales of relieved laughter, and we often talked about Merlin's adventures after that—what a character he was.

One Christmas Eve, I was alone on the farm with the animals. There was a howling storm outside; the rain was beating against the windows, and the Garry oaks were bowing and bending. I had lit the fire after the dogs and I came back, sodden, from a walk around Sandown meadow, and we were lounging in the living room. The dogs were sprawled on the sofa, and Merlin was in a big, soft chair under my pink lamp, which cast a warm glow around the room. I called Merlin a "billy dog," because he really seemed to believe he was one of the dogs—he even ate dog treats.

Suddenly Merlin let out a pitiful bleat. His eyes rolled back, and he fell off the chair and died, just like that. His lovely curled horn caught the lamp as he went down—it tore a hole in the delicate rose-silk lampshade.

I dug a huge hole in the garden that night in the teeming rain and placed him in it, as the dogs sat around and watched. Mum later did a drawing of the burial, which she called *The Death of Merlin*. She had one of my dogs looking so distraught it almost made me cry.

Until she became too frail to travel, Mum used to visit me at least twice a year on Vancouver Island. "The land of the daffodils," she'd say in a rather yearning voice each February when Fredericton was still under a heap of snow. Mum had always been a big walker, and by February she would be frustrated with Fredericton's slippery sidewalks and unplowed trails. Somebody gave her cleats for Christmas one year—spiky things that you strap onto your boots for a grip on the ice—but she could never get them on the right feet, and we'd roar with laughter when she walked pigeon-toed into a frozen snowbank or couldn't get the cleats tight enough and they flopped off right in the middle of traffic, like false teeth.

One day an old man in a Dodge Dart was driving down Mum's street while we were out walking; the snow was blowing, and it was "some slippery," as they say in the Maritimes, but Mum and I needed to get some air and thought we'd just go to the corner and back. The man pulled up behind us and yelled at Mum, "You're too old to be out alone in the snow!" Mum, who was all bundled up in her big red coat, mitts, hat, and scarf, waved at him and murmured to me, "Ignore him. He's not all there, and his wife went gaga a few years ago, poor old guy." But I was furious and yelled, "Mind your own business," and then Mum's legs glided apart and down she went, sideways, into a snowbank. We'd had a glass or two of wine before we left, and we started laughing so hard that I couldn't get her back upright. She finally made it, covered in snow, and we hobbled home, with Mum muttering, "Oh, this old age is hell—it's not for sissies, as they say." So that was why Mum often came to visit me in February or March, in the land of the daffodils, the land she loved and the place of her fond childhood memories.

Mum's father, Harold Mortimer-Lamb, was a journalist, photographer, and art collector. Harold had a nervous constitution and he found farming consoling, so he bought a lovely farm at what is now upper Oak Street in Vancouver. Mum and her half-brothers lived on the farm with their father and Mum's mother, Gran. Gran had initially been hired as Harold's housekeeper, because his wife was ill, and though they had Mum together, Gran refused to marry Harold after his wife died.

Mum and Gran would take the streetcar into Vancouver once a week to buy meat and supplies for the household. The farm had tennis courts, apple trees, and pathways through beautiful mossy woods. Mum adored her old donkey, Alice, who was best friends with the family's Jersey cow. Gran arranged grand tea parties for Harold's friends, many of them well-known artists such as Jack Shadbolt and A.Y. Jackson, which meant that Mum got to know them all as a girl. Jack Shadbolt later became her first art teacher.

Mum and Dad met in England; as war artists, they were assigned to the same studio. After the war, they got married and moved to North Vancouver, where I was born. Dad taught art, and he became good friends with the architect Doug Shadbolt, Jack's brother, who helped to design and build us a home in Lynn Valley. It was an original house, all cedar and open concept, with high ceilings and lots of light. The house appeared on the cover of a local magazine at the time. Mum saved a copy, which I have now, though it's tattered and musty. We moved to England when I was three and my brother was thirteen, because my parents were awarded scholarships to paint there and throughout Europe.

Mum felt a pull to the west coast all her life, and she was first shocked, then delighted, when I bought Glamorgan Farm in North Saanich, a large, crumbling spread that was one of the oldest farms in the Victoria area. It was a wonderful place with twelve log structures, including the outhouse. All the barns and other buildings were painted red, with red tin roofs, except for the small log house I lived in. It was set apart from the barns and down a shallow slope, in a meadow of Garry oaks. The house had coconut-and-moss chinking between the great logs, a green tin roof, and an upstairs loft containing two bedrooms with slanted ceilings and paned windows.

A gravel driveway lined with poplars wound its way from Glamorgan Road to the grandest barn and then down to the house. Laneways twisted and circled around the property, just as if it were a little town. I named each path and road after one of my friends, many of whom were writers and poets. There was Lorna's Loop, after the poet Lorna Crozier. Patrick's Lane—named for the poet Patrick Lane, who is married to Lorna—connected Lorna's Loop to P.K.'s Path. P.K. Page lived in Victoria and had become a friend by way of a poem she wrote for me about my two enormous sows, Mabel and Matilda. Poet Susan Musgrave visited, and specifically requested a swampy area be named for her. I gave her Susan's Swamp, a lush spot with thick grass and tangled blackberries where the septic-tank field was. I had signs for all the roads and the buildings on the farm hand-painted by an old hermit who lived in a trailer under some drooping cedar trees at the back of the property. He'd come with the place, and he loved puttering and decorating. He spent a lot of his time painting rocks and birdhouses and plastic gnomes he'd pick up at yard sales in nearby Sidney.

The grand barn on Glamorgan Farm, which was in the shape of a cross, had been designed and built by a Swedish work crew sometime around 1870 for the new owner of the farm, Richard John, a fellow from Glamorganshire, Wales. John had arrived on the west coast, as many others had, to seek his fortune in gold. When his gold venture failed, he bought the farm instead. At the time, the property was hundreds of acres in size. Sandown Racetrack, across the road from the farm, had been, in its heyday, a very popular venue for family picnics, country outings, and betting on horses.

I had purchased the grand old farm on the hill in 2000 on a whim. My life was at a crossroads, and I needed a change. I learned that Glamorgan Farm was up for sale, and as I strolled past it one glorious spring day with the dogs, it seemed to call out to me. The barns were falling apart, and all the fences were broken. Old cars and trailers were rusting in the bush. But the daffodils, wild in the meadow, were blooming under the gnarled, ancient apple trees, and I was seized with a strong desire to fix the place up.

By the time I bought the farm, the racetrack had been abandoned. When Mum came out to visit me, we'd stroll through the overgrown fields and around the crumbling, yellow grandstand. We discovered abandoned pear trees, along with secret daffodil woods and deer paths. Mum would gather little bouquets of flowers and paint watercolours of them at my kitchen table. We'd pick the old pears and make chutney with them.

I considered the farm a kind of trust, and I loved opening it up to the community. I held barn dances and literary readings in the high loft of the big, cross-shaped barn. Mum was visiting at the time of one such event, a fundraiser for a group that assisted sex-trade workers in establishing new lives. CBC Radio's Bill Richardson had come over from Vancouver to host it, and a few well-known poets were scheduled to read. Live music, an art exhibit, and a bar were all set up under the huge cedar beams in the great barn.

The art exhibit the group had organized featured the work of George Gordienko. That was an amazing coincidence, because George had been a great friend of Mum and Dad's when we lived in England many years earlier. George was a professional wrestler at the time, and he came over often for a drink in our little flat in London in Cleaver Square. Being only four, I called him "the man with the cauliflower ears." George had later taken up painting in Black Creek, BC, a tiny community on Vancouver Island. His work was colourful and abstract; it looked a bit like a cross between Picasso and Miro. It was wonderful for George and Mum to have a reunion.

I kept two horses on the rolling field at the front of the property, and a gardening group used another field. The group, called Healthy Harvest, consisted of seven disabled gardeners with a leader, an elderly British lady. Twice a week they came out to the farm to hoe and water and plant and till the soil, and they produced a lush, organic array of everything from cantaloupes to elongated eggplants in their greenhouse. Mum would come back from her strolls around the farm with an armload of muddy turnips or beets and a story about "those dear boys in the field." "There was one fellow who wanted to talk," she once reported. "He had a tray of baby leeks, and he said that you'd need the skill of a brain surgeon to separate them and put them into the soil. Funny fellow." For lunch, we often made soup from the tender nettle shoots that grew wild on the farm. I'd spend the afternoon cleaning, cutting, and cooking the Healthy Harvest crops while Mum took a nap.

The farm was a busy place, and over the years I filled it gradually with animals and heirloom fruit trees, rose and lilac rockeries, shady rest areas and interesting tenants—a local boat builder, a carpenter, and even a fellow who rented space to store the horrid hairy monsters and bloody body parts he used in an annual Halloween display. I strung little white lights in the trees along the driveway, and it was magical at night when they twinkled in the branches.

The house was cozy, with a stone fireplace in the living room and high white walls covered in paintings—not just Mum's and Dad's paintings, but also others I loved. One of my favourites was the giant head of a sunflower in a cheap wooden frame, which I'd paid fifty dollars for at an art show on Galiano Island.

IT WAS AN exciting event for me whenever Mum came out west to visit. I'd spend days cleaning the house in preparation. I don't think we ever stop worrying about what our mothers might think of our domestic habits. I paid particular attention to her bedroom upstairs, which overlooked the meadows. I dusted the bookcase and the dresser and straightened the candlesticks, which were wine bottles in the shape of fish from wine we had consumed on Mum's previous visits. They looked amazing, coated in drips of old, hardened wax.

I'd pick a bouquet of wild daisies from the field, or, if it was spring, some sprigs of saskatoon berry from the hedgerow, to place in a jar on Mum's dresser. Because the upstairs ceilings were on such a slant, only very small paintings could be hung on the lower part of the wall. I had tacked up posters of her favourite artists' work instead—Cezanne's apples, Bonnard's bowls of fruit, Turner's misty yellow skies, and Ensor's crowd of clowns. The Ensor poster was my own favourite of the bunch. I made sure to straighten the photos on the bookcase and dresser in Mum's room as well: her father holding a scythe in a plowed field on their farm in Burnaby; a beloved dog; John Scoones, my ex-husband, who lived on Galiano Island and whom Mum adored; and Dad sitting in his fishing boat on the Saint John River.

I'd shake out the rag rugs and place them back on the wood floor, and cover Mum's bed with Gran's thick Hudson's Bay blanket as well as a New Brunswick quilt I had brought out west with me when I left home. Mum's neighbour had given it to her, and I had always loved its traditional pattern of blue squares.

Mum always arrived on Air Canada at night after a long flight. I had the fire ready to light in the living room and a bottle of Scotch and a clean glass ready on the kitchen table for her arrival. I'd load my dogs into the van, all five of them. Mum's favourite was Havel, a strong, intelligent, handsome, and sensitive fellow who howled with delight when he saw Mum at the airport. He slept under her bed while she was on the farm and never left her side. It was a curious thing, their relationship. When Mum took a nap, Havel went up to her room with her. If she took a walk, Havel accompanied her. Whenever she sat down for tea at the kitchen table, or a vermouth on the lawn beside the honeysuckle, or a whisky by the fire, Havel hunkered down at her feet, looking up at her in adoration. I had adopted him from the SPCA, along with Gomel, a blue-eyed hound with a huge head who would sit on the arm of the couch, staring into space. "Gomel isn't all there," Mum always said. Then there were two sisters, Daisy and Lily, who had come down to the Victoria SPCA from the north. Their previous owner had died, and the SPCA advertised them as "Two Old Gals—Must Stay Together." We suspected they'd come from a trailer park, because they wouldn't climb stairs and they became animated whenever they saw an RV.

Finally, there was Alice-Mary, the Labrador I'd named after Gran. "The kindest dog ever," Mum said about her. Alice-Mary spent much of her time over at the racetrack, mooching from the old grooms who still lived in shacks behind the falling-down stables; they fed her hot dogs and let her lick the pans in which they'd fried bacon and canned beans. Alice-Mary waddled across the road twice a day to visit her friends, fellows with bad hips and hardened, calloused hands, weathered faces, and no teeth—old age as lived by a racetrack jockey.

It was an exciting moment, waiting for Mum in the airport's round "paddock area." People were there with balloons and flowers and children. It had occurred to me once that it would be amusing for Mum to be greeted by all five dogs as she staggered into the bright arrivals area. Arriving at night seems to me a bit like being born—you walk half-witted down a dim corridor after disembarking, pass a tired-looking, portly security guard, and then bang—suddenly you come through glass doors into a new world of light, activity, loud voices, traffic lights in the rain beyond the tall windows, and terrible decisions to be made, such as how close to stand to the luggage carousel. But when I attempted to take the dogs into the arrivals area, I was ordered to remove them—seeing-eye dogs only was the rule. It was just a small thing, but I often thought afterwards about what could have been. It would have been such fun to have them waiting there with me, and Mum would have loved it so much.

Even after Mum got quite frail, she still made the trip from Fredericton without assistance. "I don't trust those fly girls," she'd say about the Air Canada attendants. "They're all getting fat and old and cranky." Once I was standing in the arrivals area when suddenly two paramedics raced past the small crowd that had gathered to wait. The ambulance was outside with its red light flashing. My heart stopped—of course, I thought Mum had had a stroke on the plane or something else drastic had happened to her.

(It's always so alarming when there's an incident on a plane. One year Mum and I flew to Prague, and for some mysterious but wonderful reason we were bumped up to first class. We were enjoying the wide leather seats and liquor and cake and blankets when suddenly there was a great thud in the aisle. A large man in a suit was lying face down. The flight attendants remained calm and brought the man oxygen, and it turned out that he had only fainted. Nonetheless, Mum and I were subdued for a while, until they gave us more free champagne.)

After seeing those paramedics run by, I was relieved when Mum staggered through the glass doors, wearing dark glasses and carrying the threadbare blue nylon bag she'd bought years ago at Woodward's in Vancouver. With her full head of white hair, Mum was always easy to spot. As she grew older, her hairstyle grew more like Gran's. Whenever I first saw her, I'd think, for just an instant, that I wanted my hairstyle to be completely different from theirs when I reached old age.

Mum never brought any luggage with her. Everything was in her blue bag—two pairs of underpants, a spare white blouse, flat black slippers, a comb, eye drops, Ozonol, a toothbrush, blood-pressure pills, a sketchbook, a pencil, and one or two presents for me, usually a jar of the wild-apple jelly that Dad had made in their warm kitchen on a brisk autumn day and a jar of Lady Ashburnham pickles made by Mum. It was my favourite pickle, yellow and a little sweet and full of onion and cauliflower, with maybe a bit of carrot. Mum made it every fall and had tons of jars stored in the basement. The story behind the pickle was a Maritime one and concerned a telephone operator from Fredericton throwing her lot in with an English remittance man who had come to live in New Brunswick.

No matter where Mum travelled over the years, whether it was out west to see me or on a painting trip to Israel or on a commissioned excursion to Wimbledon or the French Open, she took only her blue bag.

Over time, the bag grew ragged and stained, and the handles frayed, but Mum didn't care. She lived in blue jeans and white shirts until she was very old, when she switched to corduroys. Her friends in Fredericton, Heather and Anne, made regular trips to L.L. Bean in Maine. They bought Mum some lovely tailored cotton blouses and sweaters, so she looked much more fashionable in her later years. They also brought nightshirts back for Dad. He was very particular, requiring them to be long-sleeved, with no collar, and made of cotton, not flannelette, with no more than three buttons and falling at least below his thighs. Dad did a funny painting of himself for Anne and Heather called *Old Geezer in Red L.L. Bean Night Shirt*. It showed him standing slightly on a slant, with skinny legs and long, bony fingers. Anne and Heather hung the painting in their upstairs hall.

I'd whisk Mum out of the airport into the mild, rainy blackness to find the van. She always said, when we got outside, "Oh, the smell of the west! How wonderful!" I agreed with her that there is a distinct western fragrance—a combination of the rain, the ocean, and the cedars.

It was a big, happy production as I helped Mum into the front seat. The dogs would be wagging their tails and panting, and Mum's dear Havel would wail with emotion. Mum would try to turn around to pat them all and calm them, but they'd be licking the back of her head and pushing against the seat, the car windows fogging up with their breath. I'd turn the defrost on high and get the wipers going in the rain, and it was such splendid chaos.

We'd pull out of the parking lot and within a minute be on West Saanich Road, almost home. A few faint lights shone across the inlet at Mill Bay. As we turned onto Mills Road, Mum would say, "Oh, there's the little Anglican church—that's where Peggy is buried," remembering an old friend who had lived in Sidney. "And Patsy," I'd add, remembering a dear friend of my own. "Oh yes, that eccentric Patsy, with her nervous, uptight husband. Remember when I gave him a painting lesson and all he could manage to do were dots?" Mum said.

Just around the corner from the municipal hall, I'd turn in to the driveway to Glamorgan Farm, white lights twinkling in the poplars that lined the driveway. I always left the porch light on so Mum could climb the stairs easily. Her Scotch was on the kitchen table; our vermouth for lunch was in the cupboard, along with white wine, made in North Saanich, for dinner. Mum and I liked to support Canadian products long before it became fashionable to "buy local."

Surrounded by the tail-wagging dogs, Mum would make her way across the porch with her old blue bag draped over her arm. "Oh, how wonderful to be here," she'd always say as I ducked in front of her to open the blue door with its sticker that said, WELL-BEHAVED WOMEN NEVER MAKE HISTORY. There'd be a cat or two on the table, probably an old cat on Mum's bed upstairs, and possibly another one on the sofa: all rescues, strays, or ferals, some from the racetrack, some from the woods, and some adopted from the Victoria SPCA.

I don't like bright light, so I used lamps all through the house. We'd cut through the kitchen, with its old iron-and-chrome cookstove and ancient, blue linoleum, to get to the living room's couch and chairs. Large windows with wide sills looked out onto the dark night meadows and, beyond that, a thick forest of firs. To the left there was a lush honeysuckle gone wild, and on sunny days it gave the living room a soft green light.

I had space in the living room for four of Mum's huge oils, all of which she had done over the years while visiting me. One was of Montague Beach on Galiano Island.

Montague is one of the most beautiful beaches I have ever seen; the azure water dazzles over the pure-white clamshell. At one end of the beach, black lava rock reaches into the sea like hard fingers, and at the other end, smooth, sculpted sandstone hugs the shore. Arbutus trees lean out from the grassy bank, their red berry clusters and white flowers dangling. Mum and I would sit on the beach on summer days with our jeans rolled up to our knees, rising occasionally to stroll or paddle. Mum usually took a swim too, no matter how cold the water was—she'd throw herself in with a shocked yelp. She never hesitated when it came to physical endeavours, though I've always been a person who stands nervously on the edge.

One afternoon Mum threw herself into the sea as usual and came out limping. "Look at my big toe!" she yelled. It was standing straight up, at a ninety-degree angle! I'd never seen anything like it, and I panicked. I wrapped a towel around Mum's foot and jumped up, saying, "I'll go for help! I'll call 911!" But Mum remained calm, sitting on a log and rubbing her foot. After a few minutes, she said, "There now, it's coming down to a normal angle." We often laughed as we recalled that day in later years. "Remember when I had that toe cramp on Montague Beach," Mum would say, "and you yelled that you'd go for help?"

Another of the paintings in my living room was a bustling horse-show scene, also set on Galiano, at the farm I'd once had there with my ex-husband, John; in the painting, the riders were all tumbling off their bucking horses because we'd let some balloons go, something I would never do nowadays because it is so harmful to ocean life when the balloons burst and fall into the sea. There was also a large painting of Long Beach on the wild west coast, shifting purple and yellow sky and silver beach—all space and air.

When Mum's eyes began to fail, she'd started to paint big spaces where she could still feel the drama. One large oil painting she did of Long Beach, which was shipped off to Montreal to sell, showed two tiny figures walking on the vast stretches of sand at sunset. Mum and I had both attended the exhibition, which was organized by her good friends and agents Eric and Alan Klinkhoff in their intimate gallery on Sherbrooke Street. The place was crowded with elegant Montreal art collectors sipping white wine, and by the time we arrived, the paintings all had red stickers on them, which meant they had been sold. Mum and I looked at the Long Beach painting and reminisced. Then she looked more closely and whispered to me, "The light's all wrong. I have it backwards. Look at the shadow—it's going the wrong way. Damn these old eyes. What was I thinking?"

She and I had a big laugh standing among all those terribly serious people investing in Molly Lamb Bobaks. We made a secret pact that if anyone ever noticed the shadow-and-light flaw, we would say that it was done on purpose, that Mum was trying to explain that travelling to Long Beach was like going back in time or something ridiculous like that. Around the same time, Mum did a painting of a hockey game, and some of the players who were whirling around the rink were missing legs—their legs stopped at the end of their big red shorts. When Mum noticed it, she asked me to add some strokes of paint, which I did.

The fourth painting I had hanging in my living room on Glamorgan Farm was of San Juan Island, a place Mum and I had visited on a road trip. This painting depicted a large ochre-coloured meadow with a grove of dark pines at the edge.

Mum always settled into the large pink chair in my living room, and before I could ask her, she'd say, "Oh, I'd love a Scotch." The dogs gathered like adoring children around her legs. As we sat chatting by the fire, my eyes would droop like Havel's from the warmth of the fire and the exhaustion of my everyday farm chores and all the cleaning and mowing and shopping and picking of flowers I had done to prepare for Mum's visit. Mum always seemed full of energy, even though she was pushing ninety by then and had had such a long journey. I'd remind her, "It's two in the morning for you!" and she'd say, "Well, I'm just so excited to be here."

The dogs went off to their beds after a while, Alice-Mary to her large basket on the porch. Because she was so portly, she was always warm. Her main goal, however, was to sleep with me on my bed. She'd pad into my room very quietly. I'd feel her big, warm head on the edge of the bed, then a heavy paw. Straining for breath, she'd haul up her huge bulk and settle on more than half the bed. I'd wake up in the morning on the edge of the mattress, with a stiff back, while she was still dead to the world, lips twitching in sleepful bliss.

Finally, Mum would decide to go to bed, and I'd help her up the narrow staircase. "We must go to the drugstore tomorrow to buy a suppository," she'd always say. "Travelling makes me so bound up." I'd make the same joke every time: "You mean the book suppository on the grassy knoll?" (A reference, albeit in poor taste, to the Kennedy assassination.) We'd scream with laughter as Mum got out the flannelette nightgown that had been in the dresser drawer since her last visit. "Damn," I'd say to myself, "I forgot to air out her nightgown," but I don't think Mum noticed during her final visits—her sense of smell was fading.

Mum always slept on top of the quilt and under the blanket, "so as not to sully the sheets," she said, "and to save you a wash." If it was a mild evening, I'd leave our bedroom windows open, and in spring there was a soothing nighttime chorus of frogs from the pond in the front meadow. A gentle sea breeze would float over the farm and combine with the woodsmoke from the chimney. "Oh, I'm in heaven, absolute heaven," Mum would call as we drifted off to sleep.

CHAPTER FOUR

I HAVE ALWAYS BEEN AN EARLY riser, and when Mum visited me on Glamorgan Farm, I'd get up especially early, just as the dawn sky brightened over the dark trees behind the house. That way, I could do a few farm chores, light the wood stove, and feed the dogs before sitting down with Mum for breakfast in the kitchen.

As I walked to the end of the driveway to get the newspaper, I would hear the waking murmurs of the chickens in the henhouse. I had two roosters, Rusty and Golden Boy, but they were dominated by a hen called Olga, and they didn't crow as often as I expected. The horses, who usually spent the night outdoors if the weather was good, would amble to the gate for their hay and feed, steam rising from their damp coats as the early-morning sun warmed them.

The feral barn cats sat on the steps of the small barn behind the nettle patch, waiting for their breakfast, but they could never be touched. The "pussy barn," as we called it, had partially restored high rafters and a wood floor. Since it had been a root cellar, it was built deep into the ground. It had a little wood stove, and on cold days I'd light a fire so the cats could gather around the heat.

And then there were my two wonderful barren sows, Mabel and

Matilda, each of them eight hundred pounds of fresh-smelling, pink, bristled, warm skin, along with their grand-daughter, Rose, and their grizzled husband, Boris, whom I had raised from a tiny piglet. When Boris was little, his skin shone like copper, and he'd run around the farm loose, squealing with delight, occasionally stopping to root in the rich black earth and clay. The gardeners would feed him roots and garden scraps and fallen apples, and Boris would chew in total delight, saliva dripping in gobs from his muddy, pink gums. Even when he grew to be over a thousand pounds of solid bone and muscle, he was a wonderful boar, always gentle and kind and not very sexual. His long, yellowed tusks could be dangerous if he prodded you, which he did mainly when he wanted a scratch. Somebody had told me to put cut-up tennis balls or golf balls on the end of Boris's tusks, but that seemed ridiculous. It was always wiser to be cautious on the farm, I'd found, rather than try to adjust Mother Nature. The pigs rose around mid-morning, or sometimes closer to noon.

Mum and I sat at the kitchen table with our toast, surrounded by dogs waiting patiently for a crust or morsel. I drank coffee and Mum had tea. "Oh, what a wonderful sleep I had," she'd say, "and dear Havel was under my bed all night—he gives me such comfort." Then, after a pause, she'd add, "I wish I had a cat—Bruno won't have any pets. He thinks they're dirty, or maybe that I'm unable to take care of a pet. But an old cat, really, it would be so nice."

I never pursued the issue deeply with Mum. We had always had pets when I was growing up. Tucked away in one of my albums, I had a photo of Mum painting at our kitchen table, with a cup of tea and a cat, a slim little tortoiseshell, beside her. Mum and Dad had a wonderful dog named Baby once too. Dad loved Baby. One time he put a white collar on her, then donned his own white shirt and tie, and somebody took a picture of them at the dining room table. In the photograph, Dad is toasting Baby, and Baby looks as if she is toasting him. But at some point Dad had decided there were to be no more animals in the house, which broke Mum's heart.

Mum and Baby flew out west, and I picked them up in Vancouver on a dark, rainy night. We missed the last ferry to Victoria, so we had to stay in a cheap motel near the ferry terminal. Our room had an orange shag carpet and brown bedspreads. Baby, who was a confident dog, marched into the room and got onto one of the beds as if she owned the place. I kept her with me on the farm after that. She was a great dog, and she lived to the age of seventeen. At fifteen, she chased a horse and had her eye kicked out, but she carried on as if nothing had occurred.

I didn't know what had got into Dad in his later years with regard to pets, but I never questioned it. The little voice in my head counselled me to remain silent. It really wasn't my business to interfere with their tensions, and the forbidding of pets was just one of many. I didn't share a tremendous amount with Mum and Dad about my own stresses and tensions either.

One of the reasons Mum came out to visit me on the farm, actually, was to have a break from Dad. But usually, within a day of her arrival, she'd sigh and say, "As soon as I'm away from Bruno I miss him—I wonder what the poor bugger is doing," and then she'd phone him. He'd never be home, because as soon as Mum was gone, Dad would head off fishing with his friends up the Miramichi River, packing the car with a cooler full of bologna sandwiches, his hip waders, and fuel for the motor on his red canoe.

After breakfast Mum and I would stroll around the farm, down the lanes and along the narrow paths I'd mowed through the grassy meadows and in between the old oak trees. As we went, Mum made comments and plans. "Oh, look, we must pick those Transparents," she'd say as we were passing an apple tree. "Oh, I must cut back that vine—it's choking the peach tree," and "Aren't these poplars elegant—we had them along our driveway on Oak Street when I was a girl."

Every so often we'd sit on a bench to rest and take in the morning. When we reached the bench beside the chicken run, Mum would say, "I must dig for those girls." She would venture into the barn to find a shovel, then enter the chicken pen. The hens gathered around her in great excitement, hoping for a succulent worm to be turned up from the packed earth. Mum would stand there in her thin white ankle socks, which were usually inside out and had fallen down around her dry, red ankles, and the stiff, old loafers she left on the farm to wear on her visits, using one foot to push the blunt shovel into the hard, caked soil. Dozens of other cracked, thin, scaly, red feet surrounded her as the chickens jostled in anticipation. We made sure that everyone got a worm, including the two downtrodden roosters. I'd collect the eggs or shovel horse manure from the field while Mum diligently completed her task.

Another pastime Mum loved was picking nettles for soup. She had shown me how to do it years earlier; you pick only the tender, new leaves from the top, and because they sting, you must wear gloves. Mum always wore rubber gloves to do the picking, so I made sure to keep a supply of the cheap yellow variety on hand. As she plucked the nettle tops, she'd place them in a chipped blue kitchen sieve that had once belonged to Gran.

On one nettle outing I noticed Mum was wearing pink rubber gloves instead. I was startled, since pink gloves were the ones I used for cleaning the toilets. "I found these under the bathroom sink," Mum said. "I didn't want to use the new ones—you should save them."

That day at lunch we had a glass of vermouth out on the deck and then ate the nettle soup we'd made. It was delicious, despite the potential for serious E. coli poisoning from the gloves. All we did to make the soup was to rinse the nettles and simmer them in water with a little salt. Sometimes we added an onion or some garlic, and then, at the end, some skim milk.

As we ate, we'd chat and reminisce. "Remember the amazing dinner that bank robber fellow made for us?" Mum said once, referring to Stephen Reid, the affable husband of the poet Susan Musgrave, who had robbed a bank in Victoria at gunpoint and then led the police on a wild chase. Along the way, Stephen had jumped out of his getaway car in James Bay, run into an apartment building, and hidden under an old couple's couch. On the news, once he'd been captured, the old couple said they had liked him, that he'd been quite well mannered. Mum loved Stephen too—he has charm. "The guy can really cook!"

said Mum, remembering a salmon Stephen had barbecued. Susan made wonderful big salads with currants and nuts and arugula before that became trendy.

After the robbery, Stephen was sent to jail, a prison on the ocean where inmates took wood-carving lessons, put on plays the public could attend, and lived together in small condominiums. Susan would tell people that Stephen was taking drumming lessons, and they'd go wild with annoyance. "Maybe I'll go and rob a bank," said my conservative neighbour, a scornful, elderly widow who lived on a sheep farm and whose husband had been an air force pilot during the war. "I've always wanted to learn flower arranging." Susan moved up to Haida Gwaii and is running a bed and breakfast.

Mum would head upstairs for a nap after lunch, accompanied by Havel. I'd hear his bones thump on the wood floor as he settled down. While Mum was dozing, I tidied up the lunch dishes and did some afternoon chores.

The pig barn was on the far side of the farm, across a grassy meadow full of buttercups, and once the pigs arose, they'd stand in the doorway, sniffing the air with their great, pink snouts for at least ten minutes, as if to test the temperature or gauge the smells of the new day. Once they'd stepped out over the ledge onto the cool earth, they would stand for another ten minutes, taking the time to wake up fully. Finally they'd grunt a couple of times and then amble across the meadow toward their feed tubs, which I had filled with warm mash, cooked vegetables (potatoes were their favourite), and apples. On special occasions I added some canned corn.

From what Mum had told me about myself as a toddler, I was similar to the pigs. I could never be rushed, she said. Once I woke up, I needed a long time in my basket to contemplate the day. We lived in Cornwall, England, then and Gran was there with us. She looked after my brother and me while Mum and Dad were off painting and sketching.

"You'd be sleeping in your basket, which we'd put in the grass," Mum told me, "and we'd hear a gurgle or two as you woke. That's when Gran would say, 'Don't rush Anny—she needs time to wake up and get her bearings.' Eventually we'd see your pink bonnet pop up, but we couldn't approach you until you were looking fully around, your little fingers grasping the sides of the basket. Then Gran would say, 'Okay, Anny is ready.'" Mum must have told me that story a hundred times, and I thought of it every time I fed my dear pigs. They would always let me know when they were ready to participate in the day.

Mum never grew to love the pigs, though. She never had the urge, as I did, to wrap herself around their lovely, soft, pink rolls. I'd scratch them and talk to them as they squealed in delight. I loved to kiss their cool, clean snouts and scratch them behind their great, flopping ears, where their hide was smooth and fresh-smelling. On hot days I'd rub sunscreen into their delicate skin.

I had another pig I kept in a separate pen. Her name was Raisin, and I had adopted her from an animal-rescue organization. Raisin was a very fat Vietnamese pot-bellied pig, a kind of small, black pig that for some inexplicable reason had become popular as a pet at one time. People in the city would acquire a pig and then abandon it after having their expensive kitchen linoleum rooted up and eaten. Apparently, one lady complained to the animal-rescue group that her pig had eaten her mattress.

Raisin had been found in a backyard in a small crate surrounded by McDonald's wrappers and Tim Hortons napkins. She was so overweight she could barely walk. After she came to live on Glamorgan Farm, she lost weight because she had a large, grassy pen to roam in, fresh air to breathe, and fertile soil to root up. Raisin had issues, however—serious ones; she was extremely bad-tempered (too much fast food, perhaps) and once bit a German woman, who was taking a tour of the farm, on the ankle. Raisin was also extremely sexual, unlike Mabel and Matilda, and she would spend hours trying to lure Boris over to her side of the meadow by leaning her portly hips and groin on the fence. Boris might have crushed her with his massive bulk, but fortunately he never took a shine to cranky Raisin, and she eventually gave up. Raisin had a lovely life nonetheless, rooting in the thistles, lying in her mud pit, and, when the weather was hot, retreating into the beautiful

Mum's sketch of "The Death of Merlin"

The completed watercolour

Mum's watercolour of our Glamorgan Farm wildflowers

Dad's self-portrait, "Old Geezer in L.L. Bean Night Shirt"

Montague Beach, Galiano Island, where Mum and I used to sit on the clamshell beach
under the arbutus tree, and where once her big toe cramped up 90° backwards!

Mum's oil of a horse show I organized on Galiano Island

Mum's oil of a hockey game in Fredericton — I painted
in some missing legs as Mum's eyes began to fail.

Various studies and sketches of my farm animals, which became illustrations
for my children's book titled *The Adventures of Merlin the Billy Dog*

Mum's watercolour of Long Beach, Tofino

2 cup JELLY JUICE
(THAWED)

PUT IN SOUTEPAN

BOIL 3 MIN.

ADD 2 CUP SUGAR
ADD 1/2 CUP LEMON
JUICE OF 1/2 LEMON JUICE

BOIL STIRING
10 TO 12 MIN.
COOL
BOTTLE -

Dad's recipe for his apple "jelly juice", written for me a few days before he died. It's more of a treasure to me than any of his art.

Dad's sketches of his fishing pals on his beloved Marimachi River, New Brunswick

Our Long Beach (Tofino) at dusk

An early etching by Dad. He loved birds.

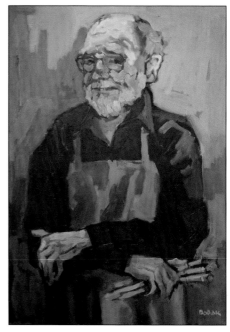

Dad's impish self-portrait,
done in his late eighties

Dad's sketch of Ottawa, done when he received his Order of Canada

Dad's sad but lovely fading tulips

Mum loved tulips. Unlike Dad, she never painted anything that was fading, wilting, or dying.

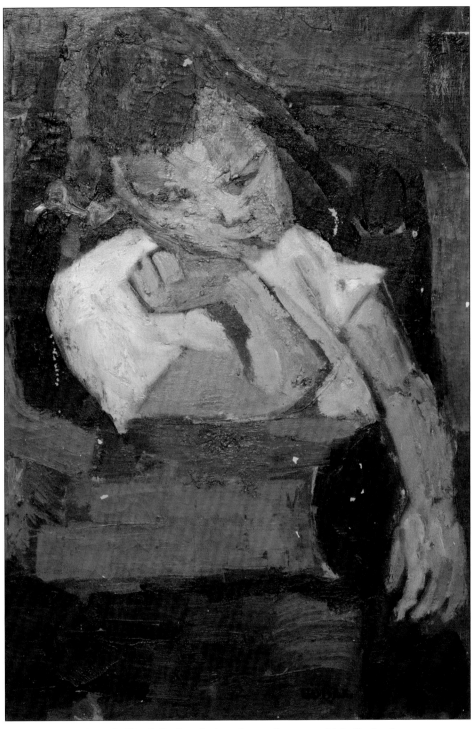

"Anny Sulking", Dad's painting of me at five years old, in England.
I remember I was bored and angry at having to pose.

Saint John Harbour at sunset. Dad loved painting the activity of harbours.

Mum jokingly referred to this painting as "the three queens". "Dick" is Dick Hatfield, New Brunswick's gay premier, and John Saunders, a gay pal of Mum who worked in the Ministry of Culture.

Two early paintings of the Vancouver Harbour, done by Dad in the late 1950s

"The Meal Parade", Mum's war art. Being female, Mum was confined to painting barrack life, but Dad and other male war artists ventured into the field.

Dad's war art—his military kit

Mum with her dog Emma; photo taken by her father, Harold Mortimer-Lamb

Mum and her best friend, Barbara

child's playhouse that the local lumber company had donated and assembled for her.

After Mum woke from her nap and we had a cup of tea in the kitchen, we'd often embark on an outing, sometimes an errand but more often a country drive or beach walk. Sometimes we'd drive into Victoria and share an enormous plastic bowl of wonton soup for nine dollars at a popular but rather dingy restaurant in Chinatown. In all the years Mum visited me, that soup remained at nine dollars, including tea and two fortune cookies, until the year of her final visit, when the price rose to ten. Even toward the end of her life, when Mum spent most of her days dozing at the veterans' facility, I'd say, "Remember that wonton soup for nine dollars?" and she'd whisper, "Oh, it was wonderful—those huge chunks of broccoli. Didn't it go up to ten?"

We always visited one of the oldest churches in BC, St. Stephen's. It was a small wooden chapel that smelled of cedar and sat in a grove of bluebells in an old orchard. Lichen hung from withered branches in the yard above the weather-beaten marble tombstones. And we'd often take the dogs to Pat Bay beach, which at low tide was covered in sand dollars and warm, shallow tide pools. To the south you could see the Institute of Ocean Sciences, with several red Coast Guard vessels bobbing at its wharf. Across the inlet were the deep-purple, forested hills of Cowichan, the place where the famous First Nation sweaters were first knitted.

After our outings we returned to the farm, where I did the late-afternoon chores while Mum had a bath and dressed for dinner—she'd change from jeans into a denim skirt she left on the farm for this purpose. She always wore her thin black ballet slippers around the house. Mum never relished warmth or coziness. She loved it when I lit the fire in the evenings, but she'd never linger in a hot bath—her baths were fast and shallow, with no bath oil, candles, or nice soap. She never wore warm woollen socks or sheepskin slippers, though I'd given her several pairs of both over the years. Even when she had the flu or a cold, she never wanted a hot-water bottle or a glass of hot rum, and she never read or drank tea in bed. Of course, she never had a massage or a pedicure or, god forbid, a facial. She came from a generation that didn't indulge in comfort but focused more on necessity.

Sometimes after supper I'd read aloud to Mum. We especially loved English and Russian history. When we discovered that the young Ivan the Terrible had thrown servants and dogs from his castle window to watch them experience pain, Mum exclaimed, "Oh, how dreadful—those Russians!" From a biography of Tolstoy, we learned that the famous writer had attempted to live like a peasant even though he was a count. He decided to go on a long pilgrimage with his farmers, wearing sandals like theirs rather than his leather boots, but he only made it a few miles down the dirt lane before he developed blisters and limped home. "What a silly man," said Mum, as the wine and the warmth from the fire began to take effect. "But oh, how the guy could write. That Prince Andrei in *War and Peace*," she swooned, "and that dear little Natasha."

AT SOME POINT, Mum and I began embarking on short road trips when she came out west to visit. My green Mazda van smelled terribly of wet dogs, but we didn't care. My friend Jane had given me a funny book with a pink plastic cover about road trips for women. The book suggested that you adopt an alias for road trips, what the author called a "road sister name." Mum and I thought this was hilarious. You came up with your road sister name thus: your first name had to be the name of the first pet you remembered owning, and your surname was the first street you recalled living on. Mum's road sister name was "Old Pup Raeside," and mine was "Gracie Grey."

Old Pup was a white bull terrier that Mum, at three years old, had had on her family farm on Raeside Avenue in Vancouver. Mum said Old Pup used to guard her by sitting with her under the apple trees. Gracie was a stray cat I had befriended on Galiano Island one summer when I stayed there with Gran and her husband, Jack.

Jack was an old fisherman from up the coast. His hands were ruddy and covered in crusty scabs from nicks he'd got from fishing hooks— that's what he told me. Jack would sit in the kitchen with his tea and scratch the inside of his ear with a wooden match. Gran and Jack had a flowering plum tree in the back meadow, and I set up a tent under it for myself using some blue cotton blankets Gran had ordered from the Simpsons-Sears catalogue.

Every morning Gran gave me a dish of milk to give to the cat, whom I named Gracie. (I am not sure why I chose that name. I found out years later that Gran's sister in England was named Grace, so perhaps I had heard it mentioned.) Sometimes I'd go into the tent where I spent the daytime hours and there'd be a dead mouse or shrew on my pillow, a gift from Gracie. By the end of the summer, Gracie was sleeping beside me in the afternoons when I had a nap. When Mum arrived at the end of the summer to take me back to Fredericton, to our house on Grey Street, I was distraught about leaving Gracie behind. So Mum and I had our road sister names: Old Pup Raeside and Gracie Grey.

Two of Mum's favourite road trips were to Long Beach, in Pacific Rim National Park, and to the American San Juan Islands, about which Mum said on every visit, "These islands should belong to Canada. What a stupid decision to give them to America just because somebody shot their pig." Apparently, on these charming islands, which are so close to us in the Salish Sea just off Sidney, a settler's pig escaped and was shot by another settler, and that set off the "Pig War," a conflict that ended with Canada losing the islands. At least, that's the story told on the plaques and display boards in the park at the fort on San Juan Island.

We liked San Juan Island because, although we could drive the length of it in forty-five minutes, the landscape was very diverse. It was wild, bleak, and barren at one end, with nothing but sparse grass and tough, dry, windswept shrubbery. In the middle were golden, rolling meadows and a beautiful coastline—that's where the forts were. At the other end, where we always stayed, there were gentle forests and a wonderful old hotel at a place called Roche Harbor.

The hotel was a crooked three-storey wooden building with worn carpets, dim amber lamps hanging from a peeling white ceiling, and huge bathrooms with tiled floors, claw-foot tubs, and porcelain sinks. The hotel was famous for having been visited often by President

Roosevelt (Franklin, I believe) as well as for being sited on land owned by a wealthy limestone-quarry owner, Mr. McMillin, who arranged to have an elaborate mausoleum built for himself and his family in the forest nearby. Mum and I had discovered his tribute to himself on a forest stroll, and it was pitiful—unkempt, due to fallen debris from winter storms, and overgrown with mosses and lichen.

The beaches in Pacific Rim Park were as beautiful as any place Mum and I had ever seen, and only a five-hour drive from Victoria—six hours if we stopped at the Clam Bucket in Port Alberni for lunch. We always stayed at a resort called Pacific Sands on Cox Bay. It was wonderfully rustic, but the suites had all the modern necessities—a patio, a fireplace, a lovely bathroom, and a compact kitchen. When we arrived, there would always be two chocolates in the shape of sand dollars waiting for us on the table, along with an emergency kit of candles and matches in case the power went out. Hanging in the closet were two giant yellow rubber raincoats for us to wear when we walked the beach during a storm.

Outside on the windswept lawn, under a grove of yew trees, an informative sign on bleached wood described the seabirds we might see on the beach. The names sounded as if they came either from an old English novel—whimbrel and dowitcher—or from a Monty Python sketch—the greater yellowlegs. There were also plovers and little sandpipers, who, in a tightly knit flock, would run furiously across the smooth sand whenever a wave washed in.

Cox Beach was the subject of many of Mum's paintings. As her sight began to fail in her later years, the beaches at Pacific Rim Park became her favourite subject. I'd take her arm at dusk after a glass of wine by the fire and say, "Come on, Old Pup, let's stroll the beach." Her canvases captured beautifully the immense, shifting gold and mauve skies over the endless silver sands, dotted with the tiny black wetsuited figures of surfers running into the grey seafoam. The scene had the energy, joy, and vibrancy Mum so loved to paint. She didn't need to see by then—she painted by sound and smell, impelled by her love of the place. The paintings from her last twenty years were bigger, with less physical detail and more space. Her watercolours were looser, with subtler colours. The people in her paintings became simply little blobs of paint, but you always knew who they were or what they were doing.

Mum's paintings were all about movement, and she was always moving herself—cleaning and dusting, walking, weeding, writing letters, washing the car, hanging out the laundry, visiting friends, having the neighbours in for tea, making bread, picking bouquets to paint. Dad, on the other hand, would sit and stare into space for hours, whether he was in his garden among the tomatoes and nasturtiums or out in his aluminum boat.

Dad's paintings had a stillness to them: portraits of Fredericton people and friends, as well as many self-portraits—I have a big oil of him looking quite impish. He would paint the New Brunswick forests and meadows at dusk, a little dead bird, a fly fisherman in hip waders standing in a slow-flowing river, contemplating his catch, still lifes of flowers and fruit spilling out of antique jugs and pewter plates.

The best example of Mum's and Dad's different sensibilities can be seen in their tulip pieces. In Mum's watercolour, a bundle of mauve and yellow tulips sits in a clear glass vase, their strong, stiff stems reaching upward to exhibit everything that a voluptuous tulip is—colour, strength, beauty, boldness, all with the delicacy of pale green leaves and tender petals. The tulips in Dad's painting are done in thick grey and magenta oil, fading, wilting, and drooping. The collapsed bouquet of grey and pink smudges may not be beautiful anymore, but they are interesting, and they trigger that little extra thought in the viewer about how the flowers used to look.

Once I picked a bunch of tall orange tulips on the farm and put them in a glass vase on the bathroom windowsill. They were stunning. But as they began to wilt, and as the colour drained from their petals, I saw that they were even more beautiful and interesting. I didn't throw them away until the petals had completely fallen. It made me realize that my world view might be more similar to Dad's than I thought.

Dad went through a lengthy phase when I was a child of painting grim, depressing-looking figures that exposed the wretched side of humanity. In some of Dad's portraits, Mum looked like death, and so did he—eggplant-coloured skin, hollow eyes, and long, bony fingers resting on sullen brown lips. Thick gobs of paint weighed down Dad's slumped shoulders—the burden of family life, of having no freedom, of being dragged down by responsibility. Even at a young age, I often felt the same. I didn't paint, though; I played with my trolls or rode my old horse to escape the kind of burden I was feeling.

Dad's gloomy paintings also included nudes—grey bodies with sagging purple breasts. A very confident girl in my Grade 7 class made it clear to the entire school that my father was a pervert who painted naked people. That was junior high, the worst time in most people's lives. In sex education we had to watch films called things like *It's Wonderful Being a Girl*, which were no match for the talk Mum and I had when she sat me down at the kitchen table one day. She drew a uterus and made the eggs look like little people who were taking a monthly vacation down a tunnel. Our principal was a pasty man in a gabardine suit and maroon tie who lectured us on the importance of having lifetime goals.

The most humanistic painting Dad did was of me, titled *Anny Sulking*. I was six years old; we were living in England, and he had made me pose in a big chair. I was furious and fidgety, and he kept telling me to sit still. I have the painting today, and I find it humorous. Dad used his great gobs of paint to give me a red eye, a slit of a mouth caused by my chubby hand sunk into my cheek, and two short, stiff pigtails. Dad's paintings were honest, and, after all, what is the use of art if it doesn't state the truth?

I've never had the courage or the desire to reveal the pains and joys of my private life as explicitly as Dad did. I once went to a poetry reading where the poets read detailed poems about their sex lives, and I couldn't bear it. Mum said to me once that art should observe carefully but not be obvious. She and I agreed on many things. We had a deep connection based on things we found ridiculous, fraudulent, compassionate, or humorous. I think that was what truly bonded us, our mutual feelings, rather than any maternal inclinations on Mum's part.

MUM AND I found the drive to Long Beach as enjoyable as our destination. We'd pack up my van with the bare necessities and then drive north over the Malahat highway. The view from the top was magnificent, with breathtaking scenery for miles. Little green farms, minuscule white ferries in their berths at the Swartz Bay terminal, small shoreline communities across Saanich Inlet. We'd drive through Duncan, known as The City of Totems. The main highway that ran through Duncan was lined with fast-food outlets and big-box stores, but farther back was a charming historical town with used-book shops, cafés, and a lovely, quaint train station. Ladysmith, farther up the road, stood on a hill overlooking a sea dotted with fishboats and log booms.

A few miles beyond Ladysmith we'd pass the turnoff for Yellow Point, a wooded area known for its lovely old lodge, which is still in operation. Mum worked at Yellow Point as a teenager, with her best friend, Barbara, and Barbara's sister, Bunty. The work sounded gruelling. They had to scrub the outhouses, clean the rooms, shuck peas, cook, and even kill the chickens for dinner. Whenever we drove past Yellow Point, Mum would always say, "Oh, how we slaved! Bunty wrung twenty chickens' necks every day, and Barbara and I had to pluck them. Our hands were raw. And one day when I was changing the buckets in the outhouse, I heard a very high-pitched English voice above me say, 'One moment, please!'"

Once, Mum told me, some guests at the lodge had gotten extremely drunk and backed their Studebaker off the hill into the ocean. "It was pitch dark, and all I could see were the headlights under the water," Mum said. But the people in the water were rescued by the other guests and dragged up onto the rocks, vomiting and coughing. Mum and Barbara had to help the impaired guests back to their rooms, bring them soup, and wash their clothes.

We always stopped for gas on our way to Long Beach. Mum loved one particular station on a wooded stretch of highway, big and clean and run by the local First Nation. It had hanging baskets of flowers, a grassy dog area with bowls of water set out, spotless washrooms, and interesting things to purchase, such as Cowichan sweaters and smoked salmon. In the picnic area, which was landscaped with boulders, a bird bath, benches, and wild shrubs, stood two totem poles, locally carved, depicting whales, an eagle, salmon, and other symbols of our west coast. A plaque described the Tseshaht First Nation culture, and I would it read aloud to Mum.

That was also the gas station where we bought Rita MacNeil, Gordon Lightfoot, and Ian Tyson CDs to play in the van on our way over the mountains to Long Beach. All her life, Mum would hum Bob Dylan's song "Blowin' in the Wind"—and then say, "That Tyson fellow was a genius."

We always had a laugh as we drove through Coombs, a scruffy, rural community known for its excellent farmers' market, which was housed in a rustic building with goats on the roof. The roof was made of sod and grass, and the goats would casually be chewing their cud in the sun or peering down at you as you admired the huge bins of local apples, corn, and peaches, and the shelves of Turkish Delight, canned Italian tomatoes, and Polish pickles. There was always a huge pyramid with jars of saskatoon-berry jam. It was delicious, and the saskatoon berry was my favourite bush. It grew all over my farm in the wild hedgerows, and in early spring it produced the most lovely white blossoms. Whenever Mum visited, I tried to have a bouquet of saskatoon-berry blossoms on the kitchen table.

In the back of the sprawling Coombs market were rooms crammed with Chinese trinkets, cheap plastic beach toys, wicker furniture, ceramic flowerpots, kitchen gadgets, and gizmos. There was a cheese counter, a butcher, and a little lane lined with second-hand shops and odd structures that looked like troll houses. Mum and I always bought an ice cream and ate it sitting under the plastic palm trees on seats that were made from sticks.

Coombs was the halfway point of our trip, and after that the scenery became hilly and forested. Around every turn were clear, cool lakes and shallow, pebbly streams. In spring, waterfalls gushing from the snowmelt tumbled off rocky ridges among the dogwoods and flowering currant shrubs. In an area of massive old-growth trees called Cathedral

Grove, people would stop and wander along the shady paths. Every so often one of the trees would come crashing down, usually during a storm, and one year two people were killed in their camper.

Sometimes Mum and I stopped at Cathedral Grove to stretch our legs, and if it was close to noon, I'd take a glass out of our cooler and pour Mum a vermouth, adding a small chunk of lemon. She'd marvel at the strands of sun filtering through the towering trees, which, I said, to her agreement, looked like a painting of the Annunciation. Then away we'd go toward the town of Port Alberni, just over the next ridge.

Port Alberni's main drag left much to be desired—car scrapyards, a Kmart, and a few fast-food outlets. At the bottom of the hill were the man-made canal, which travelled up from the sea, and the mill, the main engine of Port Alberni, which often filled the sky with white smoke and steam. We usually drove straight through town and stopped for a picnic at Sproat Lake instead. We always had a chuckle when we passed the driveway with the two massive cement lions stationed at the gate, flanked by mildewed urns full of plastic geraniums.

There was a lovely campsite with picnic tables at one end of the lake. Bobbing in the lake were the huge water bombers used to fight forest fires. We often brought egg sandwiches from home. Mum loved making egg-salad sandwiches, but her mixture was always very wet with mayonnaise, so the egg filling dripped and pulled the bread apart. Luckily, we could wash our fingers in the lake. Mum had always made bread, ever since I could remember: a brown, grainy loaf. I'd have to take big, sloppy sandwiches to school and suffer through watching other kids eating neat white-bread sandwiches that never dripped or fell apart.

At the time, I wanted nothing more than to eat "normal" food that wouldn't draw attention. Mum cooked Polish food, to please Dad perhaps, but I often opted to eat Shreddies for supper in my bedroom with my trolls. When I went to dinner at my friend Martha's house, they usually had beef and peas and potatoes, all of which I loved. Martha's family also said grace, which I never understood but loved nonetheless as part of the routine. Mum and Dad hadn't taught me any table manners, so I'd watch in awe as Martha got every last pea on her fork with her knife. I still can't do that—I prefer finger food.

I never told Mum that her egg sandwiches embarrassed me, because I didn't want to hurt her. I also ate every crumb, because I knew how much she hated wasting food. I was shocked at the way some of my classmates would throw an entire lunch in the garbage. Mum and Dad never wasted a thing; they recycled long before it became the norm. When Dad caught a fish, Mum used the bones to make soup. And Dad had the first compost on Grey Street.

Maybe it was because they had lived through a war, and because Dad's mother had had to scavenge for cabbage in the back alleys behind restaurants when his family first arrived in Toronto from Poland. The saddest thing of all was that Dad's mother, in a state of despair, had left the three boys with their father when Dad was about six. Mum told me that Dad had seen his mother waving to him through the iron gate of the schoolyard on a cold winter's day. That was the last he ever saw of her, and Dad never mentioned her to me. Dad's father had quickly remarried, a Polish woman named Mary. I called her Babi, which means grandmother in Polish. Babi and Dziadzik, my grandfather, had raised Dad and his two brothers.

Babi and Dziadzik lived on Ossington Avenue in Toronto, in a green stucco house with a front porch and a tiny back garden enclosed by tall red-brick walls. The house was dark, and it smelled of musty carpet and boiling cabbage. Babi made wonderful stewed plums. Dziadzik was big and loud, always yelling, "Hey, Ma! Hey, Ma!" at Babi. Babi just sighed and ignored him, as did I. Even as a child, I sensed he was harmless, just full of hot air, but Mum was alarmed by his yelling.

One summer Mum and Dad went to Europe and left me with Babi and Dziadzik. I had a fabulous time. Dziadzik taught me how to drink coffee. I rode the Toronto buses with him to visit his gambling pals, and he took me to a funeral home, where I saw a dead woman in a coffin. He gave me my own little watering can to help him water the cabbages in his back plot. He'd painted it green and written on it ANNY MARY.

Once Mum and I left Sproat Lake, we were on the last leg of our journey. Sometimes there was snow on the high peaks above us as we drove over the summit and along the narrow road that curved around the great rock faces. After a while the road flattened, and there was a place to park beside a rushing river with flat pinkish boulders you could walk across. That was our other vermouth stop.

Then, finally, we'd wind our way down toward the sea. The forest became sparser, the road became wider, and we'd turn the corner toward Long Beach at the information cabin. Our hearts would rise, and we'd both have a surge of excitement when we saw the huge plumes of white spray on the silver beach and heard the crash of the waves. "Oh, what heaven," Mum would gasp. Even before unpacking, we would put on the yellow slickers and walk the beach. We could hardly wait.

I took a picture of Mum one November when we were at Pacific Sands. She was lounging in a plastic lawn chair, wearing shorts, holding a glass of white wine. "Let's send this to Dad," I suggested. "He'll be so jealous!" "Yes," Mum said, "because it's freezing back there." We did send the photo to Dad, but I felt a little guilty that I had wanted to irritate him.

On Long Beach, just a little way out from shore, was a huge, ominous black formation called Incinerator Rock. Mum did numerous big oil paintings of it, calling them either *Long Beach* or *The Black Rock*. The trouble was, she had done a variety of *Black Rock* paintings that looked identical years earlier in Tel Aviv, when she was invited to Israel to paint. She loved the experience, but she described it in a way I have never forgotten. It was incredible driving through the West Bank, she said, but on one side of the road, the Israeli side, were lush orange groves growing in rich black earth. On the other side of the road, the Palestinian side, were dust and squalor and poor women clutching children dressed in rags. Mum had felt for the Palestinians.

Mum's *Black Rock* paintings from Tel Aviv were wonderful—misty ochre filled with motion, even though the main image was a rock. They were a bit like Turner's *Rain, Steam and Speed* painting of the train. Mum loved Turner, as well as Cezanne and Bonnard. Dad preferred

Edvard Munch, the Norwegian artist most famous for his painting *The Scream*. Munch's deep, sombre prints, drawings, and paintings often depicted human torment. Maybe that's why Dad loved Norway so much, because he connected with Munch. We had lived in Norway for a few months while I was a baby, since it was so easy to travel there from England. Mum told me, years later, that Dad had wanted to stay in Norway; he didn't want to go back to England or move to British Columbia. I have a landscape oil that Dad did in Norway, and you can tell he loved the country in the same way Mum's paintings of Long Beach showed how she loved the sand, the light, and the space.

The dogs were always glad to see us coming up the driveway after one of our road trips. To recover from the long journey home, Mum and I would stroll around the farm, stretching our legs, or take the dogs on a walk behind the old barns at the racetrack. Over the next day or two, we'd settle back into life on the farm.

For years, ever since I could remember, Mum's routine had been to rise early and have her tea at the kitchen table while writing in her journal (an inexpensive Hilroy notebook) and making a list for the day. She'd given up her journals as she got older; it could have been because her eyes were failing, but most likely the reason was that she no longer felt the need to write. I heard her say once, after she'd stopped painting, that she "didn't have anything else to say." I believe she was being honest with herself, and I know that she wasn't upset about it. She continued to make her lists, though, and one day I found her list, covered in toast crumbs, after she'd gone off to pick nettles. It was a feeble scrawl—"wash hair," "brush teeth," "make bed." It made me smile to see it, but I was a bit sad too.

That afternoon, Mum walked down to see the gardeners. We'd finished our lunch of nettle soup, vermouth, a big luscious tomato from the Healthy Harvest plot, and some strawberries. The dogs were lying on the cement by the deck. The pigs had gone back inside their dim barn; a breeze flowed in through the open doors, cooling their hot, dry skin. The horses were dozing under the oak trees in the pasture, and the hens were clucking contentedly on their nests. As on other warm days, the feral cats were nowhere to be seen. They were probably resting up in the dark, cobwebbed rafters, secretly peering at the world below.

The afternoon drifted gently along. When I glanced out the window after a satisfying hour of sorting twist ties, pet-food lids, corks, and broken wine stoppers in the kitchen drawer, I saw two figures slowly coming toward the house along the driveway. Once they got to the rockery of old roses and lilacs, which also held the small grave of a stillborn piglet, I recognized the two as Mum and Dale. Dale was one of the gardeners, tall, clumsy, and shaky, but he and Mum were walking in quite a comfortable fashion. I went out, and Dale said to me, in his great booming voice, his jeans all twisted around his waist, "Your mother got lost, so I'm delivering her." He gave me a little grin before he hobbled away, saying, "I have to get back to my cabbages." Mum looked a bit disheveled and seemed distant. "I should lie down," she said. I got her settled in the living room on the green couch. The light was fading, but I decided not to light the candles. Fading light would be soothing, I thought, whereas a flickering candle might be jarring in the dimness.

Mum had a little sleep under a warm woollen throw she had given me one Christmas. It had been woven in New Brunswick by a nun, and it had a beautiful loon pattern. By the time I got back from my early-evening round of chores, Mum was sitting up. "This is such a lovely room," she said. I made her some tea, always a comfort, then lit the fire.

Just before dinnertime, Mum said, "I should phone Bruno." I dialed the number for her. There was a four-hour time difference, so if Dad wasn't still at the cabin, he would most likely be watching reruns of *Fawlty Towers* and eating a grilled cheese sandwich before bed.

When Dad answered, he and I chatted for a moment. He'd been fishing all day up at the camp; he'd picked fiddleheads on a little island in the river; Celvyn from next door had come over for a beer and brought a plate of macaroni cooked by Beth, his wife. Dad loved cooking, but all the neighbours thought he was helpless and brought him food when Mum was away.

I passed the phone to Mum. "Hi, Bruno," she said. As I went into the kitchen, I heard her say, "I don't feel very well," then "I'll see if I can get a flight back sooner," and "Really? An old cat?"

After Mum hung up, she told me that someone had given Dad an old cat, and Dad had named him Ernie. She had to get back to Fredericton as soon as possible to take care of them both, she said. The real reason she wanted to leave, I thought, was that she didn't feel well, but Mum was always very stoic.

So we changed Mum's flight, and she departed for Fredericton earlier than planned. I was disappointed, and a bit worried, but not surprised. I adjusted quickly, as I had done all my life—with artists, you have to go with the flow. And as it turned out, that would be Mum's last visit out west.

In the years to come, whenever Mum was grumbling about Dad, she would say, "Remember that time Bruno lured me back to Fredericton with Ernie?" And then she'd add, "I don't think Ernie likes me—he's a man's cat."

CHAPTER FIVE

J ANUARY 2014. THE NEW YEAR arrived, and shortly afterwards fog rolled in to Victoria for a week. Archie and I could barely see the path in front of us along the beach, even after the sun had risen. One Saturday morning, after we had returned to our warm house and I was looking forward to a blissful day with books and the weekend *Globe and Mail*, I had a disturbing phone call from Kathy, one of Mum's nurses. She informed me, in the gentlest way possible, that Mum was having a difficult time. She had a fever, which made her confused, and she couldn't swallow, and she had not been able to breathe, so they had transferred her to the hospital. They thought she had pneumonia.

I called my travel agent, Susan, and booked a flight to Fredericton for the following weekend. Susan worked for a travel agency in the seaside town of Sidney, out near the airport, and through the years she had been a great comfort to me. She was always there when I needed her, behind her wooden desk covered with papers and travel magazines and the plastic souvenirs that her clients had brought her from their trips. She was a tall woman with a kind face and a positive presence, who had brought me home in emergencies, booked tickets to communist countries but warned me of the dangers, and organized my many trips back east to Fredericton. We had a wonderfully warm mutual respect. She kept my MasterCard number in her file, and she listened to and understood my stresses. Some people confide in their hairdressers, but for me, it was dear, steady Susan at her busy desk in Sidney.

I could picture Mum, so tiny and frail, with her little bent hands, under the flannelette sheet at the big German-built hospital on the hill. I called her friend Heather, who told me, "Don't worry, Anny. She's beside a window with a view of the city," which gave me comfort for a moment. Even though Mum was nearly blind, I knew she would love knowing she was by a window, thinking about the winter's purple-grey light settling over the red-brick buildings of the university and the bare trees. Both Mum and I needed lots of air and space, and we found every kind of view intriguing.

One of the first stories Mum ever told me about her childhood was the time she had her tonsils out. When she woke up after the operation in the hospital in Vancouver, a nurse brought her a dish of vanilla ice cream. Her mother arrived soon afterwards. Mum, just six years old, hadn't wanted Gran to worry, so she'd said in a rough, pitiful little voice, "I'm having a lovely time." Eighty-eight years later, she was lying in a Fredericton hospital bed with a lung infection, but she wanted to help me relax. In a strained whisper on the phone the nurse had brought her, she said, "Don't worry, Anny. I'm being wonderfully looked after. I love the hospital, and I'm on the mend."

I left Victoria under a dark sky with shifting clouds. I had packed five pairs of underpants, a warm scarf, some winter clothes, and a selection of Vancouver Island cheeses and Purdys chocolates for Heather and Anne, Mum's devoted friends. The three of us had talked about springing Mum from the Barracks after she moved there and getting her out west, but we had never been able to get the timing right. I thought I could write a story about it, called "The Abduction of Old Pup."

Getting through security in Victoria was stressful. There was a WestJet flight leaving for a Mexican vacation destination, so the airport was packed with people wearing shorts and flip-flops and carrying stuffed tourist bags. When I finally got my turn at security and crossed the yellow line, a red light went off, and I was randomly subjected to a pat-down. (If only they could do Pap tests and mammograms like that, I thought. You'd just stand there with your arms up, fully clothed, and then *click click*, all finished.) In the holding pen at Gate 10, the WestJet passengers started to get rowdy. The Toronto passengers sipped coffee and quietly read the Saturday papers, full of news about the upcoming Sochi Olympics: there were terrorist threats and protests about gay rights and the displaced, homeless citizens in Sochi.

We flew into the dawn over the many small islands below. The sky had cleared, and soon we were over the Rockies. Everything was white outside, above and below. It reminded me of a painting exercise Mum used when she taught art, exploring all the different shades of white. She'd take in props like chalk, eggs, and Gran's antique cream skimmer. Every day when she was a girl, Mum would be sent down the dirt lane to bring the family cow home to be milked. Mum's half-brother Abby would do the milking.

We landed in Toronto during a snowstorm, and I had a much-needed martini at the bar down where the Maritime flights arrived and departed. The bartender there, a woman from Jamaica, knew how to make a grand martini, I'd discovered on other trips.

The snowstorm grew worse, and the visibility was poor. Our plane sat in a lineup on the runway, waiting to be de-iced, and then in another lineup waiting to take off. By the time it was our turn to go, we needed de-icing again. We had to return to the de-icing station, where a yellow truck soaked our plane with a thick, brownish-pink liquid that coated the windows. It reminded me of Boost, the horrible stuff Dad had had to drink after his lung cancer operation.

I arrived at the Barracks quite late, but Mum, who had been moved back to her room there, was sitting up on her bed, fully dressed. She looked more frail and even tinier than she had a few weeks earlier, but she was happy to see me and very lucid. Someone had brought her a bunch of orange tulips that were just opening in the warmth of the room. A light snow was falling on the empty street outside.

We chatted, I unpacked, and a kind nurse came in to help Mum prepare for bed. She had to sleep partially sitting up now, or she'd choke, so the nurse showed me how to use the remote controls to raise the back of the bed if needed. Later, in the dark, I hit the wrong button, and Mum's legs went flying up. We screamed in hysterics, which brought on a coughing fit. Mum's choking fits were alarming. There were about ten seconds of silence when she couldn't breathe, so I pressed the red emergency button to call the nurses. They came running and slapped Mum on the back, and everything calmed down. We were told to "settle down and go to sleep," just like at camp!

In the morning we awoke to a fresh covering of snow outside the window. A nurse gently knocked on the door and asked, "Molly, would you like some booze?" Of course I had misheard; the nurse was asking if Mum would like some Boost. Now she was drinking it too. Mum had been sucking on ice chips all week, and her throat was swollen and tender, but she decided to try the vanilla Boost and managed a few sips.

I helped Mum get dressed. She could barely do up the buttons on her crisp white blouse, but finally she managed it. She combed her hair, and I brought her a warm face cloth to wash her face. It's amazing how washing your face makes you feel so revived.

We started reminiscing about the funny television programs we'd watched with Dad. There was a hilarious show called *Father Ted*, filmed in Northern Ireland. "Remember the one when Mrs. Doyle, the housekeeper, was jealous that Father Ted liked that cheap woman author?" Mum said. "Mrs. Doyle slammed the tea tray down and went on a rant, saying that the author's book was disgusting, a sin, talking all about 'feck this' and 'feck that' and someone's 'hairy arse'!"

A nurse came in carrying a long pink stick with a sponge on the end. "Now, this won't take a minute, Molly," she said. "Roll over. I have to take a swab in case Molly picked up a bug at the hospital," the nurse explained to me, and Mum said, "From my hairy old arse!" We howled, and the nurse looked horrified.

Mum drifted off to sleep again. I sat on her window seat, looking out at the snow, and had a little think. I love my "little thinks," which are just quiet moments of daydreaming, really. I picked up the expression when I was working at a school in England and we were discussing *Jack and the Beanstalk*. I asked the children, "What did Jack do at the top of the beanstalk?" and a little boy in grey shorts with chubby, red knees called out, "He sat on a rock." "And then what?" I asked, and the boy said, "He had a little think."

A man in the hallway shuffled past with a walker. He was all dressed up in a rust blazer and a tie and sunglasses, and on his head was a fuzzy hat with rabbit ears. A small lady named Kay passed by too. She always checked Mum's room to make sure Mum was okay. She told me she got so worried when she heard Mum coughing in the night that she sometimes called the nurse. Kay's son visited her often, bringing in an ambling Newfoundland dog with its pink tongue hanging out.

In the room next to Mum was a quiet lady named Dorothy, who liked to sew. Dorothy kept to herself, but for Mum's last birthday she made her a doll from black pantyhose: a monkey, actually, with a knitted purple cap and shorts and a gold necklace. "Isn't it wonderful," Mum said when she showed it to me. "The cap comes off! I was quite touched."

I wandered down to the lounge to read the local paper, the *Daily Gleaner*. The major news item was that a man from Moncton was being charged with sexually exploiting dogs. When questioned, he'd said that he "was attracted to dogs, both male and female."

Mum woke later in the morning. She tried some tomato juice, which went down well (anything but Boost!), and then a bouillon cube dissolved in boiling water, which was good too but a bit salty. We turned on CBC, which we both found good on Sundays. "There's Rex," said Mum, and an hour later, "That's Eleanor. I met her once. What an intelligent woman."

AS THE WEEK progressed, Mum seemed more and more weary, and her naps got longer. It was bitterly cold outside, but I ventured out for a bit of air and exercise nonetheless. The sidewalks were encrusted with gritty brown ice, but there was very little snow, just a dusting from one or two flurries. When Mum and Dad and I had lived on Grey Street all those years ago, I'd spent the winters playing in huge snow forts and sliding down the clean banks of snow the plows piled up on the street corners. We'd go skiing on a hill across the river under a bright blue sky. I'd fly down the hill with no poles, and then we'd take the rope tow back up. One day Mum got tangled in the rope, and it burned right through her ski pants.

When spring came, our neighbourhood would sometimes flood when the river overflowed its banks. One year we actually had to evacuate in a canoe. I'd ridden my bike home from the horse stable across town, and I was terribly excited at the drama. Dad was standing in the street in hip waders, taking photographs with one hand and holding our red canoe in the other. The water was up to his chest. I rode my bike right into the brown water, and Mum told me that I yelled, "Hey, this is fun!" Dad and his friends spent a long day and night moving everything upstairs from the basement, including a load of art. When the water receded, the basement floor was covered in two feet of thick brown mud.

One spring there was an ice jam on the river, and as the weather grew warmer, enormous pieces of blue ice floated down and landed on the Green. The great frozen chunks looked like colossal turquoise jewels, with the sun reflecting through the crystallized ice. I still remember the beauty of those massive aqua gems.

My old high school, Fredericton High on Prospect Street, was just down the street from the veterans' facility. I didn't feel the least bit nostalgic about it the day I walked by. I have only two clear memories of high school. In my Grade 10 history class, I wrote an essay about court life in France. I enjoyed doing the research and turned in a good paper in which I mentioned that because plumbing was primitive in the 1700s and people didn't bathe very often, they applied perfume to their bodies instead. I found that intriguing, but when I received my essay back from our history teacher, who dressed in brown polyester suits and had dry, scaly skin and dandruff, he had given me a failing grade, writing in large red letters in the margin beside the perfume paragraph: "You're kidding, right?" It was the first time in my life I remember being furious about injustice, because I really had researched that part of French history.

My other high school memory is rather pitiful, related to my decision to enter the Miss Fredericton High contest. I had no confidence and was not very feminine, so I don't know what I was thinking, except that I wanted to be everything I was not. (And I still do—I am simply too weary to work at it now.) I went to Woolworths on Queen Street and bought a blue corduroy dress that belted at the waist. The thing was, I also had a bit of an eating problem. I used to buy doughnuts after school at the new Tim Hortons and eat them all before riding my moped out to see my old horse, who boarded at a barn in the nearby community of New Maryland. I lumbered into my Miss Fredericton High interview feeling very embarrassed, and I didn't make the first cut.

When Mum was napping one afternoon, I walked over to the Regent Mall. It was close by, and I knew it had a bookstore and a coffee shop. I'd forgotten how depressed a mall makes me, though—endless stores loaded with cheap vinyl purses, sports stores smelling of rubber, and clothing shops displaying ugly blouses with tacky rhinestones on the collar. And then there was the food court, which I have always thought of as the most germ-infested place on the planet: all those people in lineups, coughing and sneezing over buffet counters selling noodles, barbecued chicken wings, and thick, greasy pizza. For some unknown reason, I ordered poutine from a corner kiosk that day and actually ate it. Mum's friend Heather tells a story about the food courts in Las Vegas, which are enormous. Heather was in Las Vegas on Valentine's Day—she was really there to see the Grand Canyon—and she said one of the food courts she saw was full of new brides. They threw their wedding veils and trains over the backs of their chairs as they devoured sweet-and-sour chicken on Styrofoam plates and Diet Cokes.

On a sunny, frigid day, I ventured farther from Mum's place and walked all the way down Regent Street to Fredericton's historic downtown. The Loyalist-era forts and buildings are a delight and extremely well restored. The New Brunswick College of Craft and Design is housed in a solid stone structure. Mum and Dad never taught there, as it was a newer school, but they supported it and knew all the young instructors. I went in to warm up and watched a pottery class for a while. In one of the hallways, I spotted a reproduction of one of Mum's most famous paintings, *The Queen Comes to New Brunswick*. It shows a huge crowd of people waving flags in a big green field; the queen had arrived in a helicopter.

Mum had been asked to paint the event by her friend John, who worked for the province's cultural ministry. The queen wore a royal-blue dress with matching hat, and she was led across the meadow by John and the premier, Dick Hatfield, so that was the scene Mum painted. Her friend John was gay, and so, as the public later discovered, was the premier, so Mum and John had a private joke and always called her painting *The Three Queens* instead.

One day during my visit, I suggested to Mum that I put her in a wheelchair and take her for a walk around the facility. I thought it would be a nice change for her to escape from her grey room with its fluorescent lighting and air that smelled of disinfectant.

I found a wheelchair in the hall and helped Mum into it. Trouble was, I couldn't find the brakes or the footrests, so manoeuvring poor, frail Mum into the chair was awkward, to say the least. The chair rolled over my bunion about a thousand times, and I was cursing under my breath with pain. Mum was wearing yellow happy-face socks with grips on the bottom, supplied by the facility, and her feet kept slipping under the chair. Finally, a nice nurse going down the hall found the wheelchair's footrests and attached them, and she showed me how to use the brakes too.

I pushed Mum around the hallway block, stopping after our circuit in an alcove with two blue velour couches and a television. I helped Mum onto one of the couches. The sun was shining through the windows, filling the room with warmth, and she drifted off to sleep while I watched some news about the upcoming Olympics. When she woke in a drowsy stupor, she mumbled, "Is that that beastly Putin?" Two nurses going by in the corridor were discussing Canada's women's hockey team. Mum overheard and said, "Oh yes, there's that Budweiser girl," meaning Hayley Wickenheiser.

The nurses brought Mum a lovely white cream soup and a strawberry milkshake, both of which went down smoothly. Life is truly all about these fleeting moments of joy. Mum lay back comfortably afterwards on the soft couch, with a calm throat, full of warm soup. Against a backdrop of some gentle activity by the nurses in the corridors, she dozed off contentedly.

Mum had a problem with her doctor because he was honest and blunt. "I don't need him now," she told me while we were sitting in the alcove the next afternoon. "I'm too old, and there's nothing he can do—it's too late. Whether I have cancer or the flu, there's no flesh left on me for anything to grab on to."

Just at that moment the doctor walked by, doing his weekly checks of the residents in the Veterans Health Unit. He stopped and asked, "How are you, Molly?"

Mum tipped her cup of cream soup to her mouth, swallowed, pounded her chest with her fists and said stoically, "Never felt better," which just about floored the doctor. He patted her knee and shook his head. As soon as he went around the corner, Mum had a horrendous coughing fit and almost turned purple. "Don't tell the doctor," she gasped between breaths.

Old age often forces us to be humble before we are ready. However, moments of independence can still be found. Mum was able to brush her teeth—she still had all her own teeth too—and insisted on combing her own hair. She still used the old blue comb we'd found in a lane in a torrent of rain on a Danish island many years earlier. We'd been walking in the dusk on a blustery night with clouds billowing across a navy sky. The wet black road was lined with whitewashed houses with black shutters. There was no colour, but my memory of the scene is vivid. Mum spied the comb in a gravelly puddle.

I shocked myself one day by realizing how similar I was to Mum when I scratched my nose, the way I cupped my fingers over my face and slowly stroked the bridge of my nose. It was alarming. For a moment I thought, This isn't me—it's Mum in my hands and face.

When Mum stroked her nose while drinking her white wine on the couch, Dad used to say, "Stop scratching your face, Molly!" It was just a little gesture, but it irritated him. Mum was deep in thought when she scratched her nose. It was like sucking your thumb, a soothing gesture that serves as a bridge between reality and your dream world. Dad's gesture, after tending his geraniums in the window and his lemon tree, was to sit on the couch and snort. To get back at him, I'd say in a joking way, "Dad, stop that snorting." He'd smirk and sigh.

It's funny about our physical bodies: they offer us such a picture of our humanity. Some of my strongest and deepest feelings stem from physical images. I have one that comes to me often; it's of an elderly person choosing a fruit or a vegetable at the grocery store, her stooped body leaning over the pile of produce and placing a carrot in her big, empty cart. It's sad to think that the person will shuffle home alone and cook her one little carrot.

When I got back from my daily walks around Fredericton, my face stinging from the bitter wind, I'd shuffle and skid across the parking lot, letting myself in with Mum's courtesy card to the familiar aroma of cooking and mild disinfectant. One afternoon I passed a big man with a screwdriver sticking out of his back pocket, who was mopping the floor, and the man said, "Anny?"

I, of course, replied, "Yes," and he said, "It's Bruce Harrison. I'm the maintenance guy here."

Bruce Harrison! We were in Grade 1 together at Charlotte Street School. I can still remember the first day of Grade 1; we had to sit in wooden desks in straight rows, and Bruce sat in front of me. He had blond hair that was cut very short, and he'd been so nervous on the first day of school that he'd cried and hung on to his mother until she had to leave. I was scared too, but I didn't show it. And now, years later, here he was, and when I looked closely, I could see that the back of his head looked much the same as it had then. Funny how the shape of someone's head can be so memorable.

Charlotte Street School was a lovely, old red-brick building in a charming area called the Plats, which had quiet, elm-lined streets and venerable wooden houses. I walked to school and back every day, holding hands with my friend Martha Hoyt, who lived a few doors down. When I got home, Mum would be upstairs in the attic, which she used as her painting studio, wearing her paint-smeared apron and working at her easel under a couple of bare light bulbs, dabbing on orange and red and yellow globs that would turn out to be people in coats and hats and boots, waving flags or marching or kicking a ball. I usually retreated to my room to play with my trolls.

The old school was now an arts centre with a little café in the basement. Mum and I had gone there for soup a year or so earlier, and the school hadn't changed at all. It still had wide hallways with painted, exposed pipes, tall windows, and a large, grassy play area in the back. Even the smell was the same—plaster, mustiness, and ancient dust.

Bruce was a gentle boy, and he stayed that way all through high school. He still had the same square body, but now he had a bit of grey in his hair and a grizzled beard. Every time I saw him in the veterans' facility after that, we'd exchange greetings. It was a wonderful, steadying feeling to see him strolling the hallway with his big vacuum, or fixing a light bulb, or mopping up the salt in the entrance alcove so that nobody would slip. Little, nervous Bruce from Grade 1 gave me comfort fifty years later—imagine that.

Another blizzard was due to hit southern New Brunswick. Luckily, my flight departed just before the storm arrived and closed down all the Maritime airports. Mum always said that I must have a "travel angel" on my shoulder, the way I could fly in and out of Fredericton all winter, landing right between the cancellations and the ice storms. I was zipping down to Halifax for a day before going home, and Mum and I had a final laugh before I left her in her room.

I said, "Well, I'm off to Halifax. It's still open," and Mum said, "It's a nice airport, the Stanfield Airport."

"Imagine naming an airport after men's underwear," I said, and we roared. I told her, as I always did, that I'd be back again soon and that we'd go to Shediac at the first sign of spring.

CHAPTER SIX

MUM STOPPED VISITING ME OUT west as her sight failed and she became increasingly frail. I went back to Fredericton more often instead, and Mum and I started to venture out on little road trips around the Maritimes. While we were away, Dad would usually go up to his camp on the Miramichi River to fly-fish with his friends.

Mum had never liked the fishing camp; it was a man's place, she said, where Dad and his friends drank Scotch and talked about nothing but fish while they oiled their fishing reels. The cupboards were full of cheap potato chips and stale Bugles from the Giant Tiger store, along with cans of smoked oysters and boxes of crackers. The men made crude jokes, which Mum found distasteful, and there were no books up there, she said. Nevertheless, Dad did occasionally take us up to his camp for the day. Mum and I would drink vermouth on the riverbank and dip our feet in the water while Dad checked on his canoe or the state of his smokehouse.

The younger men who went to the camp did the cleaning up and chopped fallen alders for firewood. There *were* a few books there, actually, though they were about fish. There was a silly thing on the wall, a display of fishing flies with ridiculous names such as "Gary's

Pompous Ass" or "Somebody's Hairy P . . ."—it was a man's camp, as Mum said. But wildflowers bobbed in the grass along the muddy trail that led to the water, and the slow-flowing brown river was beautiful. The setting reminded me of a Constable painting, with the sunlit foliage drooping over the water and reeds lining the river's clay banks. Fishing on the Miramichi is strictly catch-and-release, and people fish for Atlantic salmon, which are very different from our Pacific salmon. Atlantic salmon spawn in the rivers but do not die. They return to the ocean, so it is important that they are not overfished. Pacific salmon die after spawning, creating a grand feast for bears, seagulls, and eagles.

I could never understand the philosophy of fly-fishing. It wasn't about catching fish, it seemed, but more about patience and skill. Dad was very patient and very skilful, staying out on the water for hours on end. When Mum was angry with him for some reason, she'd say, "Oh, I wish that canoe would just tip over!" But of course she didn't mean it. One time, when she and Dad were alone at the camp, Dad didn't return at the usual time from his afternoon of fishing up the river. By nightfall it was cold, and Mum panicked. She trudged through the woods and along dirt roads for five miles to the nearest village, a tiny place with a church and a post office that shared a room with the RCMP. The RCMP officer drove Mum back to the camp, prepared to search for Dad and his supposedly overturned canoe, but there Dad was, sitting by the fire with his Scotch and his Bugles, furious that Mum had left the camp and "caused a scene."

The first eastern road trip Mum and I embarked on was to the Digby Pines, an elegant Canadian Pacific hotel in Digby, Nova Scotia. The car I rented at the Fredericton airport was an Impala—Mum and I called it the Impaler. In preparation for our trip, we packed the blue cooler with ginger ale, vermouth, and egg sandwiches. We had a big argument with Dad at the house first, because he wanted us to use up the bologna that was in the fridge for our sandwiches, and we wanted egg.

"Why don't you take the bologna to the camp?" I asked Dad as he was folding his hip waders into the back of his car, but I received no answer.

Mum said, loudly enough for Dad to hear, "Just pack the damn bologna—we'll feed it to the seagulls in Saint John Harbour."

Dad ordered, "Don't use my white bread," and Mum said to me, "Bruno likes his enriched white bread—it's like eating cotton wool." Dad gave me one of his famous looks of exasperation, in which his lips got thin and twisted, and he let out a sigh.

The three of us had had a big argument about food on one of my earlier visits to Fredericton too. That time, Dad had arranged to drive Mum and me up north to a windswept New Brunswick island called Miscou. It was a beautiful place. The cool autumn temperatures were turning the shrubbery from a lush green to a dry gold. Miscou felt abandoned; a few lonely, boarded-up summer cabins sat looking out at the cold Atlantic. Much of the island was a rust-coloured peat bog, full of wild blueberries that we gathered in baskets Dad had brought along. The pebbled beach was a deep red. Mum and I waded into the surf while Dad started a fire in his portable barbecue—and then the tension began. Dad had packed "boil in a bag" dinners (wieners in a plastic bag) that he had bought at a discount store in some mall in the suburbs of Fredericton. Mum had brought along homemade hamburgers, which she had mixed with Dad's homegrown onions. A storm came up while Mum and Dad were arguing about what to eat, and a ferocious wind blew our paper napkins onto the beach. As I remember, we ended up eating canned tomato soup at a damp turquoise motel a few miles along the highway from the bridge to Miscou.

Once things grew quiet after the bologna-and-white-bread faceoff, Old Pup and Gracie hit the road, taking the scenic route along the beautiful Saint John River. We had decided to stay at the Hilton in Saint John for the night and catch the ferry that crosses the Bay of Fundy to Digby the next morning. Ideally, a road trip provides you with a breath of fresh air, a break from whatever makes you tense in your everyday life. I was always a bit more high-strung than either Mum or Dad, however, a little more nervous, so as we drove, I was fretting about obstacles Mum and I might come across, such as the toll on the bridge going into Saint John. How much did it cost to cross? What if I didn't have the exact change?

What if I got into the wrong lane? Worst of all, what if I had some sort of problem that caused me to hold up traffic and got me into trouble? All my life I have stressed about getting into trouble. I'm a good citizen—I pick up beach litter, I volunteer for the Parks department, I help people in all kinds of ways—and yet when I see a police car behind me, I always pull over, assuming I'm the one they're chasing.

Another worry I had was about putting gas in the car. I never pump my own gas in Victoria—it's dirty, and I also have this colossal fear that the gas won't shut off and it will spill all over the place and cause a disaster and the gas station will blow up. I had to keep reminding myself, "For goodness' sake, Anny, this is the Irving Big Stop gas station in the middle of New Brunswick, not the Tokyo freeway." Mum and I always had some wonderful moments on our road trips, and some hilarious ones, but generally I felt a little stressed that something would go wrong, or that I would look like an idiot, or that I would get lost or take the wrong turnoff. Needless to say, my nerves were frayed by the time we reached our destination. Two or three martinis would help with that.

I'm ashamed of my nerves, embarrassed that I have never conquered them. Many events in my life would have been more fun, more blissful, if I had been more relaxed. Mum said once, "I don't know where your nerves come from—from Dada [her father] perhaps, or from your Polish side of the family." I seem to be able to control my nerves better when I'm alone—I am able to think more rationally then. It occurred to me recently that perhaps Mum made me nervous on those road trips, as much as I liked travelling with her, especially when she was humming "Blowin' in the Wind" and saying how much she loved that Ian Tyson.

The country road along the Saint John River wound its way through rustic New Brunswick villages, rolling meadows, farmland, and marshes full of water birds. One brochure I picked up described the Saint John as "The Rhine of North America." Mum and I howled at this. "More like the Volga," I offered once we'd settled down. I meant it to be flattering—the Volga is the same deep-brown colour as the Saint John and about the same width, with lovely villages, churches, and bathers along its grassy banks. One difference is that on the Volga's banks, there are small, onion-domed churches in among the thick lilacs.

There's something lovely about a river—it's gentler than the sea, and interesting succulent plants can grow along the banks. Mum had once been asked to paint a very rare plant for a collector plate. The plant grew only in a particular spot on the Saint John River—it was found nowhere else in the world. It was delicate and wispy, with minuscule yellow flowers and thin stems. Imagine that little plant choosing this one spot on the entire planet to thrive. Unfortunately, it didn't have a very attractive name—it was called Furbish's lousewort.

Mum and I made our first stop in Gagetown, even though it was only twenty minutes outside Fredericton. My nerves needed a rest after driving through a suburb called Oromocto, which had a big roundabout that hadn't been there the year before. Gagetown had stately old wooden homes along the river, a post office, a town clock that stopped at 1:46, a small museum, and a pottery shop. Mum and I often drove there for an outing when I was visiting her in Fredericton, and every time we did, I visited the pottery shop to buy some of its green pottery with a fiddlehead motif.

Mum thought pottery and gift shops were passé. "It's all been done to death," she'd say. And she didn't like the fiddlehead design on the mugs and plates I'd collected from the Gagetown shop. That afternoon I bought a fiddlehead-pottery toilet-paper holder, but I kept it a secret from her—it really would have made her squirm! I carried the bag to the car, but when she asked, "What's in the bag?" I said, "Oh, just a little Gagetown gift for my house-sitter—a soap dish," and to further underplay it, "A trinket from New Brunswick." I felt compelled to lie, but I experienced some regret that I couldn't share my joy of buying something I liked, something that made me happy, with Mum.

It had to do with taste, of course. Mum and Dad had taste, especially Mum. Her father had been an art collector and a photographer, who displayed Asian jade sculptures and carvings, Persian carpets, and Group of Seven paintings at his lovely home on Burnaby Mountain.

His wife Vera, Mum's stepmother, was slim and elegant and wore expensive silver jewellery.

Dad's taste was more original. He made furniture, especially tables, that he designed using motifs from nature. His tabletops were tiled patterns of wild birds or clay mouldings of reeds and grasses. In our house on Grey Street, Dad had covered the dining room ceiling and walls with gold cigarette papers—Peter Jackson—then made a papier mâché cherub and hung it from the lamp. He did things like that. His taste wasn't intimidating, just unusual and quirky. Mum's taste was intimidating, though, and I was nervous about my own taste being unacceptable. For example, Mum hated gladioli and dahlias with a passion—she thought they belonged in funeral homes—so I never bought them, even though we lived five thousand miles apart.

Mum and I progressed along the river road, chatting about the new slogan that should go on New Brunswick licence plates. A provincial competition for the slogan was under way, and Mum and I decided, as we passed grassy ditches and meadows of blue lupines, poppies, clover, and buttercups, that maybe New Brunswick should be called "The Wildflower Province." Because so many people don't really think about New Brunswick, "The Forgotten Province" was another one of our ideas.

The Saint John River has many lush green islands on which farmers put their cows to graze during the summer. The animals are easily barged across from the farms that line the riverbanks. But as we drove, Mum and I saw a barge that had somehow gotten wedged in the heavy river mud. The poor cows were stranded in the middle of the river with only their calm, soft heads visible above the water. Farmers and backhoe drivers and local helping hands were trying to pull the animals ashore with big ropes. I'm sure it all worked out well, and it was a fascinating thing to see—like a rescue at sea.

On the approach to Saint John, the riverside road wound out of the rolling meadows we'd been driving through and onto a wide, marshy plain. In the hazy distance was the Bay of Fundy, and in the foreground a four-lane highway curved toward the toll bridge that led into the city. Smokestacks spewed white steam from the Irving pulp mills.

Saint John gives off an interesting energy, rustic Maritime charm mixed with a big-city feel. Mum often reminisced about the time she'd been invited down to Saint John to meet Prince Charles and Camilla. Dad refused to go—he went fishing—so Mum's neighbour Beth drove her down. The two of them dressed up in their nicest clothes—Mum wore her grey woollen skirt, a white blouse, and the green glass beads I had brought her from Mexico—and they headed off "to meet the prince," as Mum said. Mum reported later that Camilla was charming—they had discussed the fog that had rolled into Saint John that morning and the rain in Britain. Beth added that Camilla was very down-to-earth. Charles was "a dear," according to Mum. He and Mum talked about watercolour painting, and apparently Charles was extremely articulate on the subject and genuinely interested in Canadian art.

A massive sign on the highway just before the toll bridge indicated the way to the Reversing Falls. Mum and I always chuckled at the whole idea; the "reversing falls" were actually just a few yellowish-brown rapids that churned and swirled at the end of the river, where it emptied into Saint John Harbour. They only reversed when the tides changed.

Mum and I were booked to stay at the Hilton Saint John, a modern brick high-rise on the harbourfront. The Hilton was a magnificent treat, and we liked it so much we made it our own escape on the road trips that followed. We felt as if we were miles from anywhere, even though we were only seventy miles downriver from Fredericton. We were at the gateway to the world, it seemed—there was a view of the misty sea from our room on the fifth floor, which had free bottles of shampoo, two big, comfy beds, and an ice machine down the hall for our vermouth. We seemed to be the only people in the hotel (except for one year later, when there was a New Brunswick pipefitters' convention), which contributed to the luxury.

We entered our room using a card that slid into a slot. Mum marvelled during our stay that we could actually open the door "with a bit of plastic," though I was always nervous it wouldn't work. The first thing I did was pull the big brown upholstered chair and footstool over to the window. I sat Mum in it and poured her a vermouth. I decided to order a martini with pickled onions from room service.

"Go ahead," Mum said. "I think I'm a millionaire—I just sold a painting."

After a nap, we went out exploring. I took Mum's arm as we strolled up and down the hilly streets, breathing in the sea air, which was pungent from the pulp mill. We admired the brick factories and stone churches with red-painted doors and ornate iron gates. Mum loved the streets and hills and the old brick neighbourhoods of Saint John, and she had painted those themes many times. On the lower streets, we encountered a humorous public art display by an artist named John Hooper. He had carved rotund figures of people out of wood and then painted them. The people were doing everyday things. There was a mother holding a baby, a businessman in a suit and tie reading the newspaper, an ugly little girl screaming as she held a lollipop. Mum and I wondered why she was screaming, and Mum said that maybe it wasn't a lollipop she was holding but a mirror, and we burst out laughing. The figures were so lifelike, you thought they might speak. Mum sat down on the bench beside the woman with the baby and told her how sweet her baby was. Next she sat down beside the woman in a yellow dress, who was looking lonely and clutching her stomach. Mum tried to offer some words of comfort. The show was very clever and sad and funny as well.

After socializing with the wooden figures, we decided we'd each have a bath. "Use lots of hot water," Mum advised me. "Mr. Hilton's paying for it!" We had a glass of white wine in the Hilton bar afterwards, and then dinner. Mum had seafood soup with a bun, and I ordered steak and dessert—a piece of McCain cheesecake. I ate as if it were my final meal. After dinner we ambled along the Hilton's patio, set above the choppy brown bay, and commented on the evening skyline: a row of smokestacks, steeples, and red-brick chimneys. The only spot of colour in the fading grey light were the pink petunias in a few cement planters.

Dad had once done a painting of Saint John Harbour, looking out to sea at dusk. Grey silhouettes of cranes, tankers, and warehouses were washed in a fading, golden ocean light. He'd actually painted it from the Hilton's eleventh-floor suite. Dad loved painting harbours—the business and activity of them, as well as the serenity, the rugged tugs and tankers tied to the docks under a night sky, waiting to depart at dawn. I have three of his harbour paintings hanging in my home in Victoria: a large dark oil of the Thames in London at night, and two colourful, rather abstract pastels, one of Vancouver's harbour and one of the harbour in Victoria.

I love harbours too—they are so romantic, and they are filled with so much motion and anticipation. When I was in my early twenties, I was travelling through Sweden with a theatre group, and I went for a walk along some shipping docks one misty evening. A grey ship tied up there was called the *Gdansk*. I was entranced. Having been raised during the Cold War, I'd come to believe that the communist countries were faraway and mysterious lands, although I always knew they weren't "evil," as Ronald Reagan described them. Maybe because Dad was Polish and I spent time with my Polish grandparents in Toronto, from a young age I felt able to understand and relate to the Slavic temperament—rough but sensitive.

My empathy and wonder grew so immense that when I was ten years old, I sent a letter to the Kremlin. I told them I knew Russians weren't evil and that I'd love to visit their country. I wrote the letter in secret—I didn't tell Mum or Dad or anyone. By ten I had already developed a secret life of sorts. I didn't want anybody to know anything I was doing, ever, and I was slightly embarrassed about my letter as well—I worried that people would think I was crazy to try to make friends with Russia. I addressed my letter to "The Kremlin, Moscow, Russia."

About two months later I came home from school to find Mum smoking a cigarette at the kitchen table and writing in her journal as she drank a cup of tea. She announced, "Anny, there's a parcel for you from Russia." I grabbed it and went straight to my room. Mum never asked what it was; she must have understood that my Russian obsession was an extremely private affair. I opened the parcel, and in it were masses of little books, posters, and pamphlets on Russia, some written in awkward English and some in Russian. As far as I could see, the topics ranged from the grasses of Siberia to Soviet-built transport trucks. I was ecstatic—nobody had ever given me this kind of attention. My heart now belonged to the Russian people. The paper in the booklets was thin and the coloured ink blurry and faded—so different from our paper and printing, which made me love Russia even more. And there was a letter! It was from someone Russian who thanked me for my interest and said one day he hoped I could visit his great country. The trolls set about building a mini-Kremlin in my bedroom, and after that I'd sit beside it, playing my tape of the beautiful Russian national anthem on an old tape recorder Dad had given me.

AFTER A COMFORTABLE night on the crisp, tight sheets at the Hilton, Mum and I embarked on the second leg of our journey. We drove back over the toll bridge and through west Saint John, a very old neighbourhood with parks, slanted houses (slanted due to their age and built on a hill), potholed streets, and churches. The famous citadel stands stoically on a high hill overlooking the bay. Mum and I drove up there and took a walk around. I always read information plaques wherever I go. I read the citadel plaque aloud to Mum, who stood there not paying much attention, and then we headed back down the hill to the Digby ferry dock. Mum always called the ferry, the *Princess of Acadia*, "an old Irving rustbucket," but to me it was an adventure. While we waited for the boat to dock, we skimmed stones, flat black pieces of shale embedded in the red sand, into the water.

The ferry came in, a slim blue vessel that opened like a big mouth at the front. We drove on into the dark hull that smelled of fish. Before we went above for the three-hour crossing, I poured us each a small vermouth. I had swiped two pieces of lemon from the Hilton bar the night before, and we sat there in the Impaler, on the lush velour seats, sipping our drinks as workmen hosed down the cold steel lower deck.

Mum had good strong legs right up to the time she went to the veterans' facility, so she could easily climb the steep, rusted stairs to the lounge and cafeteria two decks above. We shared a tuna sandwich and a pot of tea, then went out onto the front deck. A deckhand offered to take our picture as we settled onto a freshly painted white bench in the sea breeze and left Saint John in the distance.

Later, Mum dozed in the lounge while I wandered the ship. I read information posters about sea life and visited the gift shop, where I bought a pair of lobster socks for Elizabeth May. Elizabeth had become a good friend when I lived on Glamorgan Farm in North Saanich. She was a Maritime girl, so I thought she'd appreciate some lobster socks from the *Princess of Acadia*. I bought an Ashley MacIsaac CD too—he plays the fiddle like a maniac but is so talented. Rita MacNeil had him on her Christmas show once, and I'll never forget it, this young, wild boy dressed in baggy jeans and a T-shirt, dancing and playing his fiddle with so much energy that his bow strings were spiraling into the air.

The approach to Digby was truly lovely. Mum and I went outside again to watch as the boat proceeded up the inlet past green hills dotted with little white houses. Once we landed, we set off for the Digby Pines, which turned out to be a wonderful place. The entrance was up a wide driveway with a woodland on one side and a grassy slope on the other. The slope was planted with tall, elegant pines whose long needles shivered in the breeze. Our lovely room, up one flight of a carpeted spiral staircase, had big windows we could open, and it overlooked the wide lawns and gardens below and the sea beyond. The furniture was dusty-pink velvet, and the curtains were lace. The lamps had cream-coloured silk shades.

In addition to the blue cooler stashed in the back seat of the Impaler, Mum and I had brought fresh underwear in an NB Liquor bag, along with our toothbrushes and Mum's eye drops and blood-pressure pills. Mum's eye drops were a complex business. She had three different kinds, and they had to be given to her three times a day in a specific order. Dad had written down the directions for this on the back of an old Christmas card from the Mulroneys, the former prime minister, Brian, and his wife, Mila. Mum and Dad had received Christmas cards from the current prime minister ever since they'd each been awarded the Order of Canada. In the photo on the Mulroneys' card, one of the Mulroneys was holding a baby, and the whole family was wearing navy-blue sweaters and white shirts, or white sweaters and navy-blue slacks. The instructions about Mum's medications were in Dad's neat block printing: PURPLE CAP, THREE DROPS BEFORE BREAKFAST—WHITE CAP, THREE DROPS AFTER 15 MINUTES—BLUE CAP, THREE DROPS AFTER 15 MINUTES. NO BLUE AT LUNCH—REPEAT AT DINNER TIME. DON'T FORGET GREEN PILLS.

The "green pills" were calcium, which Mum threw down the toilet every morning. "I don't need calcium," she told me scornfully. "I was raised on Jersey cow milk!" It was true—she still had all her own teeth, and strong bones too. I had also been instructed by Dad to make sure Mum took her daily pills from the bubble pack that had all her pills organized for one month; they were arranged on a grid, like a calendar. Every day you were supposed to pop a bubble and then take all the pills in that bubble. The trouble was that Mum couldn't see, and I'm slightly dyslexic and can never read directions. I gave Mum her pills on the horizontal grid of days when I was supposed to be following the vertical days. Dad almost killed me when he learned later that I had mixed up the grid pattern. Once we got home, Mum and I had to walk to the Sobey's pharmacy, along the railway tracks and across town, to buy a new bubble pack of pills.

We thought it was hilarious, but Dad was furious. He even called us "dumb broads." "You dumb broads can't even count across to seven," he said. Mum and I both thought that people were overmedicated, anyway. We'd read in horror that female whelks in a bay in Victoria were growing little penises from ingesting all the hormone medications that were flushed down toilets and then dumped into the ocean. The whelks couldn't release their eggs because the little penises were blocking the way. This is what drugs can do—it's a serious issue. One day, if we don't watch out, we may all be hermaphrodites.

Mum and I agreed that the cure for many ailments was to go outdoors and forget your aches and pains. Mum never wanted to get a flu shot, even when her weight dropped to ninety pounds. Her attitude frustrated Dad—he was far more trusting of and reliant on the medical profession.

Whenever Mum and I needed to stretch our legs at the Digby Pines, we'd amble through the grounds, following short forest trails, admiring the beds of lilies and roses, and passing under the arches of gnarled fruit trees. Every so often we'd sit on a wooden bench to rest and reflect on life—people we had met, poems and books we loved, and memories we had.

We thought we were in a Henry James novel. Everything was so peaceful, so articulate and graceful. I felt as if we should have parasols! We chuckled about how much we'd loved Colin Firth as Mr. Darcy in the latest film of *Pride and Prejudice*: "That Mr. Darcy made the whole of Fredericton swoon," said Mum. Then she added, turning sombre and a bit melancholy, "Our neighbour, poor Miss Ames, bought the DVD. All her life she was a schoolteacher. She lived all alone, across the street from us. She'd putter in her garden, and we'd have lovely little chats. Then, just as she retired, she got lung cancer, and she had nobody to help her. I sometimes sat on her steps with her as she was going through her chemo treatments. She had lost all her hair and was so tired, and she cried. But Mr. Darcy gave her some joy at the end of her life." We were silent for a moment, thinking about Miss Ames, and then Mum continued, "Oh, how I love England."

"Me too," I said.

"Bruno can't bear it," Mum said. "He loved Oslo, and Spain, but he detested England, and England didn't like him. I remember him carrying his satchel of pastels around to the galleries and being continually rejected. There was one arrogant gallery owner who, after looking through Bruno's work, said with his nose in the air, 'Too blue for my stable.' Imagine! Poor Bruno."

"Why do you think people are drawn to certain places?" I asked Mum. "Why do I love England so much, and why am I so drawn to the Slavic countries? Is it because of genetics, do you think? I feel such an enormous pull to those places."

Mum was quiet, and then she said, "Oh, the English can be so funny."

Whenever I was visiting Mum and Dad and there was tension—some little thing like when Mum left the birdseed out and the squirrels spilled it all over the deck, or someone cut the cheese on an angle (me), or Mum and Dad were out of onions—I'd suggest that Dad put on a *Fawlty Towers* or *Father Ted* episode, or Mum would say, "Let's watch Mrs. Bouquet!" from the program *Keeping Up Appearances*. Dad had taped them all, so he'd put one on and the three of us would have a drink and scream with laughter when Mrs. Bouquet (Hyacinth) fell into the bushes and got her dress caught in the roses, or when the German guest came to stay at Fawlty Towers and poor Basil hissed under his breath, "Don't mention the war!"

We always watched the Royal Canadian Air Farce on Friday evenings when I was there, howling when Luba Goy did Elizabeth Taylor, and the other woman did Liza Minnelli, and the chubby fellow did Stephen Harper like a robot, with that shiny-lipped grin. We loved George Carlin too. We agreed he was a comedy genius. In my view, one of his best lines was "The reason they call it the American Dream is because you have to be asleep to believe it." Imagine the courage it took to say that in the United States in the 1960s. And one time Mum had a coughing fit laughing at Little Ronnie James as he described how he'd held in his gas on an Air Canada flight en route from Thunder Bay to Winnipeg. "And then I let it go on the landing!" he said in his funny, manic way. Why *is* it that we get such painful bloating when we fly—is it the change in air pressure combined with bland Air Canada coffee?

Digby is a delightful village with one main street and several restaurants, all of them advertising FRESH SEAFOOD on painted sandwich boards. We settled on the Captain's Cabin. Mum had the pan-fried haddock with cooked carrots and mashed potatoes, and I had a plate of the world-renowned Digby scallops. We shared a bottle of Jost wine, a very good Nova Scotia variety.

We took a walk on the wharves as dusk descended. Fishboats bobbed in the chop, firmly tied to the creaking docks. What a joy it was afterwards to get into our beds at the Digby Pines with their soft, white duvets. I'd brought along Samuel Pepys's diary, and I read an amusing entry he had written about marital trouble. He'd had a joyful day and then gone to bed with his wife. She promptly fell asleep, and he had a dream that she "had lain her hand on his cockerel." Mum and I had a big laugh about that, and she said in her Cockney accent, "'Ow disgusting," as we drifted off to sleep.

On our third morning at the Digby Pines, Mum and I decided to make a day trip to Yarmouth, down the coast a little way. It was a stormy day with a howling sea wind, but we set off anyway. Mum was game for anything, and I had suggested we try to locate the tallest wooden church in North America, which was supposed to be in one of the many Acadian villages along the shore.

The Acadians originally arrived on the east coast from France in the 1600s. Their lives were not easy, and there was a massive expulsion of them by the British in later years. Some of them retreated to Louisiana. The Acadian anthem is *"Ave Maris Stella"* ("Hail Star of the Sea"), and their flag is the French Tricolour plus a yellow star. Their villages remain active communities along the Maritime coastlines, and the Acadians speak a distinct French dialect, quite different from the French you hear in Quebec. I always love driving through Acadian towns and landscapes. As a people, they are a rich part of Canada's heritage, and they amazingly have kept their own culture.

When you stop at an Acadian café for a bowl of clam chowder and a bun, a lobster roll, fried clams, or a fried piece of cod, the people are down-to-earth and friendly. The cafés usually have plastic tablecloths and a simple menu, but the food is delicious. Enjoying a bowl of hot soup and a piece of cream pie in an Acadian village on a stormy day in Nova Scotia, with rain pounding on the windows and spray blowing up from the ferocious sea, was a wonderful experience. Mum and I did find the tallest church too. It was right on the road, painted grey, and in front of it sat a weathered and worn statue of Mary in an oval shelter surrounded by a halo of burned-out light bulbs and plastic flowers. The church was beautiful inside, glowing with white candlelight. We were greeted by a quiet teenage boy dressed in a white shirt with a red sash who was selling postcards and fridge magnets.

MUM AND I made several road trips to Digby after that first one, always staying at the Digby Pines and sometimes travelling on from there. One year we drove east along the Bay of Fundy, marvelling at the endless wetlands stretching into dark forests on one side of the road, and murky water lapping onto a ribbon of red sand on the other. It was autumn, so there weren't many other visitors when we got to our destination, the Annapolis Gardens. The maintenance people were busy raking and cleaning up the site for winter, but we enjoyed seeing all the trees and flower beds and looking out over the marsh that stretched to the bay. "I like the marsh better than the gardens," Mum said. "It's more interesting, and it's where Champlain stayed when he mapped Nova Scotia. That was after he almost died while wintering in New Brunswick on those islands at Saint Andrews." Mum was a big reader, and she knew so much. As we stood in the knot garden, a fenced-in square where the shrubs were clipped perfectly to form a large knot, Mum added, "You know, the Mi'kmaqs helped him, and those dikes in the marsh were built by the Acadians."

One year, to our great dismay, the Digby Pines was closed for renovations. After much discussion, we decided we should stay in a bed and breakfast in Digby instead, and I selected one called White Caps by the Sea. It was on the main street in a big, old wooden house, and what fun it was. The hallway was packed with shelves of knick-knacks, huge gold vases filled with plastic flowers, rubber fruit, antique furniture, mirrors, statues of Venus and Zeus, and lobster memorabilia.

Our nice hostess served us sherry in the lounge, which was jammed with overstuffed red velvet furniture, stacks of travel magazines, ceramics, lamps with fancy shades, pillows, and stuffed toys. Her husband had just made cheese biscuits, which he brought out on a silver tray.

Mum and I really had a chuckle when we saw our beds. They looked like something Henry the Eighth might have slept in—great wooden headboards, heavy red quilts, and six pillows per bed, sheathed in red velvet pillowcases with WHITE CAPS written on them in gold embroidery. Burgundy draperies with gold cords hung from the canopies, enabling us to close the curtains around each bed. Breakfast was amazing—more cheese biscuits, pancakes, muffins, eggs, and a ham. Mum reached for a bunch of grapes hanging from a massive centrepiece, but they were rubber, and she almost pulled the whole display over. Our host sliced the ham—this was his moment of glory.

That afternoon on a walk around Digby, Mum and I reminisced about a bed and breakfast we had once stayed at in a village in northern England. The host, a big man with a red face and a grey, bushy beard, came out of the kitchen sharpening two long knives, followed by his wife, who carried a huge, fatty ham. As he sharpened his sabres, he announced, "We will now say grace." He thanked God for the ham, and the pig, and the pig farmer, and the pig farmer's wife, and the farmhands, then the butcher in the village, then the butcher's wife. As his grace went on and on, Mum and I got the giggles. All the while he continued to sharpen his knives, and behind him his wife was drooping, sagging, and perspiring from holding the enormous ham.

Mum and I were on a three-week road trip around England, and I had foolishly decided we should take the scenic route from the airport at Heathrow to our friend Joe Plaskett's house in Suffolk. Joe was a Canadian and an old family friend, an artist who had a second home in England.

It would have been far easier to drive to Joe's house on the motorway. Instead, Mum and I spent hours going at a snail's pace through tiny villages, past old stone grain mills, and along muddy country lanes. At one point, we seemed to be going around in circles. "Didn't we pass that thatched cottage an hour ago?" Mum would ask. Finally, we stopped to rest in a place called Saffron Walden, and when I spotted a postman, I said, "Mum, run ahead and ask him how to get back to the motorway." Mum ran after the postman and tripped and fell. I felt terrible, but she bounded right back up, calling over her shoulder, "It's these damned shoes from Zellers. The soles are loose!"

Somehow we made it to Joe's place by suppertime. He had a lovely old home on a bit of land between a goat farm and a cow pasture. The goats came to the fence to be stroked. Joe's house was musty and cozy, full of paintings and marble sculptures, lamps with glass shades, and antiques.

We sat out on his patio, enjoying English Stilton cheese and wine, and later Joe put on some Chopin as we sat in the living room, surrounded by pewter candlesticks and plates of fruit. (Real fruit, in his case.)

Joe had done a series of paintings showing dining room tables the day after a dinner party, and Mum bought me one as a present. It's a treasure. The table is covered with a blue-and-white tablecloth, and on it sits a green wine bottle, some empty wineglasses, a basket of half-eaten bread, and a slender silver vase of purple flowers. Morning light leaks in from a narrow window. Joe might have done the painting in Paris, where he had an apartment for a while.

Mum and I both loved Stilton, and before we flew back to Canada, I bought a large round of it—a real stinker, very blue and aged. Stilton is a delicious old traditional cheese with a thick brown crust around it, like an old toenail—you don't eat the crust, but it preserves the cheese. We put the cheese in the overhead compartment on the plane, planning to split it in the Toronto airport before I headed on to Victoria and she flew back to Fredericton. As we were over Greenland, the cheese began to smell, and its odour permeated the cabin. Mum and I were aghast, but neither of us said anything, and later we made it through customs easily. I'm not sure we were really allowed to bring a big, stinky cheese across the ocean, but we did!

MUM AND I adored Nova Scotia, but one year Dad persuaded us to take a road trip to Shediac, a town near Moncton, instead. Shediac is close to the bridge that takes you to Prince Edward Island, and very Acadian. We set off on a spring day with our cooler of egg sandwiches and our vermouth. We had decided to go via Saint John, driving to Shediac along the southern coast.

As usual, we passed through Gagetown, where we stopped to rest and I bought another piece of fiddlehead pottery—a toothbrush holder this time, again in secret. Mum would have been appalled. At Saint John we turned off and were soon in Sussex, a lovely town with an old railway station. The landscape wasn't as rough and wild as other parts of New Brunswick, but tame and lush and green, with tidy fences around rolling pastures, and contented, grazing cows. Little farmsteads with white wooden houses, red barns, and pretty flower gardens dotted the countryside. They make a delicious cheddar cheese in Sussex, and it's not stinky (like that Stilton).

Farther along, we arrived at the Hopewell Rocks, huge red rock formations on the beach that have been worn by the sea and wind into great arches and other shapes. To our dismay, however, we discovered we had to *pay* to see them. Buses carrying schoolchildren and tourists were lined up waiting at the gate. Mum said, "Imagine having to pay to see a couple of rocks!" so we drove on.

The road climbed a hill, and as we came down toward the sea, we reached a pretty village called Austin. The place was just a few motels and cafés along the road and a wharf where some local fishermen were organizing their nets and traps. We saw a sign that read BEST SEAFOOD CHOWDER IN THE WORLD, so we stopped. The chowder was truly delicious, not too creamy or thick, and we sat beside a sunny window and watched the red waves washing onto the beach. Mum and I both had a moment of total inner happiness then, I think.

As we proceeded along the coast, the landscape changed completely, becoming a vast expanse of wild marsh with not a house to be seen. But then, curiously, we came upon a winery. A small sign read WELCOME—COME AND TASTE OUR WINES, so we drove up the gravel driveway to a tidy hut, where a friendly lady welcomed us in. We did indeed taste her wines, which were all made from fruit. Mum sat on a stool and sipped a bit of each one, and we bought a bottle of the blueberry. We learned later that fruit-wine production was a new and booming business in New Brunswick.

We continued along the highway until we reached the turnoff for Shediac. As you enter town, just before crossing the bridge, you pass the "World's Largest Lobster." It's in Rotary Park, and according to the brochure, it weighs ninety tons. People get their photos taken sitting in one claw beside a carving of a fisherman wearing a yellow sou'wester.

I had made reservations for us at a century-old inn called the Tait House. It turned out to be large and elegant, tastefully painted a pastel green, with a lovely, mowed lawn and shrubs. To get to our room we climbed a flight of wide carpeted stairs with a beautiful stained-glass window on the landing.

Shediac is well known for its long, sandy Parlee Beach, so Mum and I decided to take a walk by the sea. A late-afternoon breeze came up over Northumberland Strait. Across the strait, we knew, was Prince Edward Island. We took off our shoes and eased our feet into the freezing salt water. Mum and I always had the urge to plunge our feet into the ocean, wherever we were in the world. Dad had no desire, ever, to wet his feet.

Back at the Tait House, Mum and I settled on the beds in our sunny room to have a glass of wine. Mum had a bath, and then we went down to the dining room for dinner. We were the only people there except for a man in a green shirt who sat alone in the corner, looking at a newspaper and picking at a salad. Across the hall in the lounge, men in business suits stood around drinking and talking in groups, looking important. It was the weekly meeting of the Shediac Rotary Club.

Mum said to me, "Have a martini—you love martinis," so I did, with olives. Mum stuck with wine. "A nice Canadian dry white," she said when she ordered. The waitress brought us a basket of bread and some little balls of butter. Mum and I began to feel pretty good after our day of driving and our beach walk. We had a simple dinner as taped music played in the background. The Rotary men had left by then, and Mum began to hum "Moon River" along with the tape. That was the first song I'd ever heard her hum, when I was about six years old, and now here she was, humming it in the Tait House and swaying to the tune.

Then the most extraordinary thing happened. The man in the green shirt approached us and asked Mum to dance! Mum roared with laughter before stumbling to her feet. Her sight was failing, and it was dim in the dining room, and she could barely stand because we'd had too much to drink, but the lovely man propped her up as she draped herself over his wide chest, and they went twice around the tables. I took a photograph, and when it was developed, Mum and the man looked like a big orange swirl. All we learned about the man was that he was attending a conference in Moncton and that he was from Dartmouth.

I told him Mum was an artist—"One of only three living Second World War artists," I said proudly. Dad and Alex Colville were the other two.

Mum and I stumbled up the staircase to bed. After we brushed our teeth, I opened the window and a cool breeze blew in as we climbed under the thick duvets on our soft beds. "Oh, that was a wonderful day," Mum said.

"And what a way to end it," I exclaimed, "with a dance around the Tait House with a total stranger."

Mum murmured, "If you ever write another book, Anny, I hope you call it *Last Dance in Shediac*."

I said, "I will. Good night, Old Pup."

Mum's father, Harold Mortimer-Lamb. Mum said that
he took to farming after several nervous breakdowns.

Gran and Mum

Mum as a young artist

Mum with her donkey, Alice

Private Lamb

Mum as a young war artist

Mum and Dad as young war artists

Dad and Mum, early days in England

Mum in her attic studio in Fredericton

Dad in his new Fredricton Studio at the University.
He set about drawing portraits of everyone he met.

My best friends in Clever Square, London, early sixties

The three of us in the house that Dad designed and built with
Ron Thom and Doug Shadbolt in North Vancouver, about 1960

I was in a major snow battle with my neighbour Martha Hoyt, but I stopped to smile for the photographer before smashing Martha's fort to smithereens.

Dad encouraged me to paint, but alas, I was more drawn to writing.

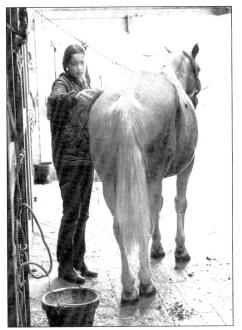

As a young teenager, my old horse Missy became my life.

Mum on Landsdowne Street with Shep and Birtha (who was neurotic), Fredericton

Mum at her kitchen table at her favourite house on Landsowne Street, Fredricton

Late November, Mum with her vermouth at Cox Bay, Tofino, our favourite road trip destination. We sent this back to Dad who was in waist-deep snow, but he never responded.

Dad toasting "Baby" one New Year's Eve

Mum in repose for a magazine article

Mum on one of our road trip picnics on the side of a
New Brunswick country lane, with Vermouth, of course

Mum and me in Saint John on the harbourfront, en route to Shediac

Last Dance in Shediac

CHAPTER SEVEN

T HE NEXT MORNING WAS CRISP and sunny. Mum and I
took a drive up the eastern coast from Shediac to a village called
Bouctouche, which was the birthplace of K.C. Irving. Irving is a
big name in the Maritimes. The family is into oil and gas stations and
should not be confused with the McCains, from Hartland, who are
famous for their potatoes and frozen cream pies. Bouctouche sounded
quaint and charming, and there was much to see, according to the
glossy brochure we picked up: the Irving Guest House; the Irving
Waterfront Park; the Irving Memorial Chapel; the first Irving oil and
gas station (now a historic site; it first opened in 1924); the K.C. Irving
Statue in the main square; the Irving Memorial Gardens; and the Jean
E.S. Irving Plantation.

Much to our delight, the area along the rugged, red coast was
Acadian, dotted with village churches, fishing boats, and stacks
of lobster traps on mowed lawns. The star flag flapped in the sea
breeze, and across the strait we could see lines of windmills on Prince
Edward Island.

Our specific destination was a mile-long boardwalk built by the
Irvings—the Irving Eco-Centre, which stretched out into the ocean

over seven and a half miles of tide-washed sand. At the entrance was a nature house full of plaques and brochures on shore life and the marine habitat. Mum and I sat on a bench while I read to her about the plight of the piping plover, an endangered bird that lays its eggs right on the sand in the grassy sand dunes.

It was one of those wonderful, sunny salt-air days. The breeze blew gently, the gulls glided above us, and the waves were quiet on the red sand. I read aloud to Mum from a brochure about the local creatures with shells: "The lady crab is grayish to yellowish with purple specks, and hind legs flattened like paddles."

"That's useful, for a lady," Mum said in her funny Cockney accent.

I read out the parts about the slipper limpet and the mud dog whelk while Mum sat listening in her sunglasses with the pink lenses. We always joked about her "rose-coloured glasses."

We walked far out to sea on the boardwalk, arm in arm, then returned barefoot on the beach. The beach, being on the open strait, was littered with ocean debris—shells and sponges and interesting seaweeds. When I got back to the car, we drove farther up the road to have lunch in a place called Rexton. I ordered yam fries, which I constantly crave, and they came with a roll and butter. That was so Maritime, to serve a roll and butter even with yam fries. Mum had homemade chicken soup (and a roll and butter).

We stayed at the Tait House one more night, though the man in the green shirt had departed. By the next morning, a storm had come in. Mum and I dashed across the parking lot and into the Impaler under a piercing rain, and I turned on the heat along with the window wipers. Off we went, driving on the newly paved highway from Moncton back to Fredericton.

We arrived home by noon. Dad had beaten us there, and he was filleting a fish in the kitchen sink. Mum and I laid the table for lunch. It was such a different world from a few hours earlier in Shediac. To cope with the change, Mum and I had a vermouth in the living room while Dad continued to putter in the kitchen.

I always loved Dad's lunches—he'd put out little patés and cheeses, and slice a red pepper as delicately as he painted a violet. My favourite thing was his cucumber in dill and vinegar. He'd peel the cucumber and slice it lengthwise, then place the slices in a little dish and soak them in white vinegar, salt, and dill.

After lunch, Mum and Dad would both head upstairs for a nap. I'd do the dishes, then sit and read. When Mum woke up, we'd usually go for a walk along the river. Dad kept busy with his bird feeders, his plants, or his sketches for the rest of the afternoon. Sometimes Heather and Anne would visit with their dogs, Sophie and Arthur, around tea time, or Beth with her little dog, Millie.

Dad would offer the dogs Milk-Bones from a crystal dish I'd brought back for him from Belarus after my disastrous visit there. I'd brought Mum some Belarussian rubber boots, made in a village factory. The boots were thin and not very warm, but Mum loved them and wore them with thick woollen socks. If it was chilly, Mum would also pop on the "llama hat" I had sent her one Christmas. It was made with wool from a llama farm near Victoria, and it was like a security blanket for Mum as she got older and felt the cold more. She always said, "Where's my llama hat?" when we were getting ready to go outdoors.

I craved five o'clock at Mum and Dad's house, when the wine or martinis would be brought out. Once darkness fell, Mum and I would take one last walk along the river or around the block under the tall elm trees, reflecting on things we'd seen or done that day.

"Oh, wasn't the Tait House wonderful," Mum said on our evening stroll the day we got back from Shediac. "I wonder what the man in the green shirt is doing tonight?"

"Maybe watching *Wheel of Fortune* on television back in his apartment and eating a TV dinner," I suggested.

Sometimes on our evening walks in Fredericton, if Mum wasn't too tired, she'd suggest we go one more block, past our old house. "That was a lovely place," Mum would say, pointing to it. "Remember the wonderful studio I had in the attic?" Mum and Dad had purchased the house on Grey Street after we'd rented in the neighbourhood for several years. I had two particularly vivid memories of the Grey Street house. I was nine years old when we moved there, and I had more than thirty trolls, all of which I adored. My life was my trolls, in fact, and I had my entire bedroom set up for them—split-level houses, swimming pools, a whole troll town. One Christmas, somebody gave me a Barbie doll and a Ken doll. I despised them. The trolls hated them as well, so they installed a torture device on the windowsill. Barbie and Ken were lowered naked out of the window on ropes tied to their hair, left to dangle until the trolls cut the ropes and the pair fell to their death on the street below.

My other vivid memory about the Grey Street house was the time Mrs. Michener, the Governor General's wife, came to the house to buy some of Mum's paintings. Before I went off to school that morning, Mum warned me not to come home after school unless I was prepared to be polite and to curtsy to Mrs. Michener. I didn't think too much about it. I had my horse, Missy, stabled across town at the old Wilmot Downs racetrack, and I usually went to see her after school. So that afternoon, like most afternoons, I went to the crumbling barns to clean out Missy's stall and ride her up in Odell Park. I loved the racetrack; it was home to many haggard grooms who drank whisky until they passed out in their little rooms in the barn lofts, but they were all kind to me. They'd tease me and call Missy an old nag; they smelled of tobacco and pine tar and fresh hay. I forgot all about Mrs. Michener, and after my ride I just wanted to get home, grab the bowl of Shreddies I usually had for dinner, and watch *Silent Night* (a soap opera) in my room with the trolls. I rode my battered CCM bike across town, following the railway tracks, and then up Grey Street. Parked in front of our house was a big black limousine with Canadian flags on the hood.

I stormed into the house, smelling of manure, with filthy hands and boots, wearing a huge, dirty, turquoise Linus sweatshirt. Mum and Mrs. Michener were having tea in the kitchen, I remember; Mrs. Michener was wearing a beige camelhair coat, belted at the waist. "Anny, this is Her Excellency Mrs. Michener," Mum said. I knew I was supposed to hold out my hand and say hello, but something got hold of me, and I scowled at Mum and said, "Her *what*?" Mum would tell that story in hysterics years later, but it was very rude at the time. To make things worse, my neighbourhood friend Martha Hoyt came over a few minutes later, all dressed up in a pretty dress, and as I spied from the stairs, I heard Mrs. Michener say to Martha, "You may kiss me," and Martha did! Martha curtsied and kissed her hand! I was incensed, and I locked myself in my room with my trolls until I saw, from my window, the limousine leave. Then I went down to get my Shreddies. Mum never punished me, but I'm sure she was mortified.

"Those were good days," Mum always said when we passed our old house on Grey Street. I had mixed feelings about the house myself. Our years there were a productive time in Mum's life career-wise, but junior high school was not pleasant for me. I was in an uneasy transition period, that strange stage when you don't really know who you are, when you are leaving childhood behind but are not yet aware of it.

Kitty-corner to our old Grey Street house was a large, elegant wooden place painted white with black trim, with an enclosed glass porch. "There's Nan's house," Mum always pointed out. "Poor old Nan; her last year wasn't terribly joyous. She was a spinster, you know. She lived there with her sister, and some young man took advantage of her at the end. She was such a bright woman—we had great conversations over tea. One time she brought over a friend, a thin, nervous woman who ate all the cat treats on the coffee table, thinking they were snacks. I didn't have the heart to stop her. Bruno was furious, not because the woman had eaten the cat food, but because I had fed Puss on the table!" The story made us roar with laughter every time. "Poor Bruno," Mum would say, wiping her eyes. "He's just too clean. What's wrong with a bit of cat hair?"

As our stroll continued, we would pass a neat barn-shaped house, white with green trim. My parents had rented it the year I was seven. The white house was owned by the Smiths. Leonard taught classics at the university, and he and Barbara and their son, Timothy, who was my age, had gone to Greece for a year. I have a horrific memory from that place, something I didn't tell anyone at the time for fear they'd think I was crazy. My bedroom was upstairs at the front of the house. My bed sat under the window, and it faced the doorway; beside the doorway was an old tea-shipping crate full of my toys. The hall was just beyond.

The ghost began appearing almost as soon as we moved in. Almost every night when I went to bed, no sooner would Mum turn off my light than a terrifying man would appear in the tea box. He was naked, and I could see him only from the waist up; he'd grin at me but never speak. He had a bushy, red handlebar moustache, a hairy chest, and a very red face. I wanted to call for Mum, but I was struck dumb with terror, even though I could hear Mum's and Dad's voices downstairs.

I began to have terrible dreams of huge green balloons. In the daytime I threw ferocious tantrums—I remember tossing a chair through the window and tearing up my bedsheets in an out-of-control rage. I beat up Martha Hoyt a few times too, in the sandbox. My tantrums grew so frightening that Mum and Dad took me to a child psychologist at the university. I was an astute little girl, so I sensed that this nice woman was not just showing me ink drawings as a friend. I knew I was being analyzed in some funny way, so I decided to give only vague, short answers.

The ink drawings were in the shape of male genitals. When the psychologist asked me what I thought they were, I said they looked like giraffes—a giraffe reaching for a leaf, a giraffe drinking from a pond, a giraffe between two rocks. I remember that as clearly as I remember the man in my toy box. When we moved out of that house, all was calm, and I never saw the hairy, red, naked man again.

It sounds as if I imagined him, but I am sure he was real. I still believe he was a bad ghost or spirit. Whenever Mum and I walked past the white house at night, we could see the fluorescent glow of a television in the upstairs bedroom that used to be mine—the haunted room. Someday I'd like to go back into that room and curse the spirit that—although it couldn't break me—frightened me nightly. I'd like to go back and face it, to shake my fist at the spot where it used to appear and say, "Begone, ghost!"

By contrast, I had a wonderful experience with ghosts when I lived on Glamorgan Farm. When I first went to look at the old farm, it was rundown and abandoned, but something attracted me to it. The log house was dark and drafty, as I'd expected. I next checked the great barn and walked slowly up the stairs to the loft. Of course, it was dusty and full of cobwebs and bird nests. A bat even flew past, which didn't scare me at all—bats are extremely shy and useful creatures, consuming numerous harmful insects. As I was standing in the centre of the loft, a warm feeling passed through me, a gentle, happy type of energy, and it was in that instant that I decided to purchase the property.

I thought nothing of the experience until a few months later, when I was giving a tour of the property to a preschool class from Sidney. I took the kids up into the loft, where we sat in a circle and chatted about farms. Suddenly one little boy went and stood at exactly the spot where I had been when I'd had the warm feeling. The other children climbed back down the ladder and went out into the sunlight, but this little boy, aged four, sat down in the spot in the loft and said, "I feel nice here. There's a ghost, but it's a nice ghost."

I couldn't believe my ears! But as life went on, I started to notice that the dogs would go up into the loft and lie on the special ghost spot every day. One day, a man who had cared for the cows on the farm years earlier dropped by to visit. I invited him in for tea, and as he looked out the living room window to where the green coolness of a wild honeysuckle was sprawling all over the side porch, he asked blandly, "Have you met the ghost yet?" I believe in ghosts now, and I think in my life I have met an evil ghost and a lovely, kind one.

Continuing on our jaunt, Mum and I would walk a little farther, rounding the corner and heading down Alexandra Street toward the university gates. "The Mockler twins lived there," Mum would say as she pointed to a nice house, and then, "There's Judy Budovitch's house. What a lovely person she is, and a good friend—she's done wonders for the art gallery." Through the years I'd met Judy many times; she'd come over to Mum's for tea or invite us to her place, and she was so kind and calm and steady. After Mum moved to the veterans' place, Judy gave her a purple quilt that Mum became very attached to. Whenever I'd tuck her into bed, she'd say, "Where's Judy's quilt?"

When I was growing up, Mum and Dad's friends Don and Lydia

Kasianchuk lived in a small stone house across the street from Judy's. Don taught engineering at the university, and Lydia sang with the university's madrigal singers. I remember them well from those days, mainly because of Don's appearance—he had a brush cut and looked exactly like a well-known wrestler, Gene Kiniski.

I was obsessed with live wrestling at the time. The main Maritime wrestlers were The Beast and his brothers, the Kay Brothers, and their opponent was The Stomper. Live wrestling was broadcast on television from Halifax every Saturday afternoon. The Beast was short and muscular and very hairy. The Stomper was taller and bald and mean. I loved The Beast and hated The Stomper. One time, Mum took me to a live wrestling show at the Beaverbrook Rink, just down the street from our house. It was packed with people drinking beer and smoking, and in later years Mum would fondly recall me quietly rooting for The Beast as The Stomper was kicking him in the head over and over again. The poor Beast was tangled in the ropes, and apparently I kept leaning forward and murmuring, "C'mon, Beast, c'mon, Beast—kill him, Beast."

One day a new wrestler came to town—Gene Kiniski. Gene brought Bulldog Brown, a horrid, pale little man with a twisted mouth, with him from the west. And then a wonderful thing happened. The Beast and The Stomper became friends and formed a tag team to fight the intruders. The Stomper pummelled Bulldog Brown, and after that I loved The Stomper too.

Lydia and Don eventually moved to Victoria, into a lovely home full of art near the sea. Now they have become *my* friends. They look exactly as I remember them from when I was eight years old. Dear Don still has a brush cut!

When Mum and I returned from our nightly walks around the neighbourhood, Dad would still be up, puttering with his fishing flies or his plants, or making soup for the next day. Mum was usually ready for bed, so she would go upstairs. I would stay up with Dad for a while in the living room, having one more glass of wine and maybe watching another episode of *Fawlty Towers* with him. There was nothing much to say, but it was nice to spend that time together.

ONE OF MUM'S favourite places to go to on a road trip was Saint Andrews, a charming little town on the sea about seventy miles south of Fredericton. Sometimes we'd go down for lunch, and other times we might stay the night.

I knew from stories Mum had told me that when Gran came to Canada from Canterbury, England, as a young woman, she settled first in Saint Andrews and worked as a gardener. That was before she went to work as the housekeeper for Harold Mortimer-Lamb and his family. The family lived in Montreal then and later moved to the west coast.

Gran pined for Saint Andrews all her life, Mum said. Mum had adored her mother but at times was affectionately critical of her. "Mum was never quite contented," Mum said on one of our late-night walks around the neighbourhood. "She was always angry at somebody or something, always fighting a hopeless cause. Poor old Mum." Almost every time we visited Gran, she would, at some point, say to Mum, "Molly, I'm just one big fraud." It bothered Mum to hear her mother say that. Being so young when I spent time with Gran, I didn't realize that she was sad, filled with regrets, and pining. I think now it took a certain amount of courage to admit such a thing, especially to her daughter, even if I'm not sure exactly what Gran meant.

Mum herself always pined for the West, "to come back home," she'd say in one of our quiet evening moments on our road trips, but in another breath she'd wistfully recall that her happiest times had been in Saint Andrews at the Gleason Arms, or skiing under a moon along the river in Fredericton. Perhaps longing is simply remembering a time long ago, and nothing to do with contentment.

Mum never confessed too much to me, though perhaps she tried and I diverted the conversation. Mum and I shared a sense of humour and a compassion for things, but not deep personal emotions—she had hers and I had mine. I'd built up some comforting walls with my trolls when I was very young. When Mum was in her seventies and still visiting me on my farm in North Saanich, I knew she was worried about her state of mind. Sometimes she'd forget things or get confused with directions. I think now that she may have had a mini-stroke or two. At the time, she'd say, "Sometimes I think I'm losing my mind—do you think I am?" And I'd say, "No, Mum, losing your memory is not losing your mind." I wish now I could have given her more comfort, but I didn't know how.

Gran never cared a hoot for money or material goods. There was a hilarious story about Gran and an A.Y. Jackson oil painting that went like this: When Gran finally left Harold, in a bit of a huff, she took a small oil painting by A.Y. Jackson off Harold's wall. It was a winter scene of Quebec, with a dark purple sky and a few dark trees and rolling, snow-covered, distant hills. It had been painted in the 1920s, at the height of the Group of Seven's fame. Gran moved to Galiano Island, where she set up a small inn called Arbutus Point. She needed a carpet for the entrance hall, and one day, on a whim, she traded the A.Y. Jackson for a threadbare red rug.

Some time later, Harold asked for the painting back, to put it in an exhibition; he told Mum, who was at art school in Vancouver by then, that it was one of the best pieces A.Y. had ever done. Gran panicked and called Mum. "Molly, what should I do?" Mum told her not to worry, that she would ask A.Y., a family friend, to do a replica, and nobody would ever know. A.Y. obliged, and Mum presented the painting to her father. Harold, as an avid art collector, was an expert—he had supported the Group of Seven as well as Emily Carr. Mum said he took one look at the painting and gasped, "This isn't the same painting at all. My original was done in 1925, and this was done recently."

Years later, the replica ended up with me, and I sold it through a local art gallery. It wasn't worth as much as I thought it might be, because it had been done later in A.Y. Jackson's life, and apparently that had an enormous influence on its value. I often wondered who had bought the replica and thought how much fun it would be to tell them the story of Gran and the threadbare rug. Then one day a good friend and I were having lunch, and she said, "My friend Hugh, a retired dentist, just bought a beautiful A.Y. Jackson." It turned out that the painting was indeed "mine." Not only that: Hugh had been my dentist when I was a teenager. He had advised me then not to have any teeth pulled or to get braces to treat my sore and cracking jaw. He said I'd grow out of it as my jaw matured, and he was right—what a good dentist! And now I knew that he collected art too.

Once, when Mum and I went down to Saint Andrews for the night, the car-rental company at the airport gave me a car called an Enforcer. The Enforcer was bright red with a "spoiler," a great red, shiny shelf contraption on the back to make the car go faster. "Look, Old Pup," I said to Mum when I got to the house, "a hot rod!"

The next day, Dad went to his fishing camp, and Mum and I drove the Enforcer out of Fredericton on the Hanwell Road, which soon went from passing strip malls and car dealerships to winding through scrubby countryside, wild meadows, and marshes turning auburn and ochre with the change of season.

The first village we came to was Harvey Station, which has a train station, a corner store, and several churches. As you enter town you see a grand old red barn, and on the lawn next door is "The World's Biggest Violin" and a plaque stating that Harvey Station was the home of musical legend Don Messer.

Mum and Dad and I had a good friend who lived in Harvey, Steven Fletcher, a beloved hospital worker who cared for sick children. Steven's father had been the doctor in Harvey, and his brother owned the insurance company. Steven lived in the family house, right across from the giant violin, with his old dog, Lah Lah, and two sweet rescued cats, Tommy and Callie. Steven was on the Harvey Beautification Committee, and he had a beautiful place on nearby Harvey Lake as well.

Steven's cottage was small and cozy. He kept it warm by burning alders in the wood stove. Steven had glass jars of jujubes and red licorice on every table, and the walls were covered with prints of Dad's work. Sometimes Mum and I would drive up from Fredericton to spend a day with Steven at the lake. He'd cook a huge casserole or make a potato salad, and we'd sit out on the deck beside the lapping water and drink wine. And whenever we went to Saint Andrews, we always stopped in Harvey on the way through to visit Steven and Lah Lah and Tommy and Callie.

Saint Andrews was delightful, with one main street along the water and shops that sell locally made woollens, soap, and knick-knacks. Mum and I always had lunch at the Lobster Corner, which served delicious lobster soup. But the highlight for Mum was really a memory of Saint Andrews—the year she'd stayed at an inn called the Gleason Arms and written a book. She once told me that that had been the happiest time in her life. "How I loved Mrs. Gleason, the owner," she'd recall, "and her hairy old dog, Panda. I'd write and walk and sketch, and then have a sherry every evening with Mrs. Gleason. How kind she was." The Gleason Arms was still there, an old white building on the water with a barbershop downstairs and apartments upstairs, and every time Mum saw it, she sighed and said, "Oh, the dear Gleason Arms—what wonderful memories I have of it."

Mum's book was called *Wild Flowers of Canada*. "Stupid title," Mum scoffed. "It had nothing to do with flowers. It was about my life, but the illustrations were my flower paintings." Mum claimed writing that book was the most difficult thing she'd ever done. Her writing style was completely different from mine. It didn't go into detail about either her life or her thoughts. Still, I asked Mum once what she would have done had she not become an artist, and she said she would have liked to be a writer. I think there are some deep differences between the two kinds of expression, but one thing writers and painters have in common is this: there are days when it just "won't happen" and other days when things just seem to flow. There were days when she stared at her canvas and nothing happened, Mum said, and other times when "something floats by and I can catch it." Once I started writing things down myself, I understood what she meant. For me, if I don't catch the floating thought I hate myself, but Mum never hated herself—she told me that. When she stopped painting in her old age due to her failing eyesight, she didn't grieve, either, but rather resigned herself to the situation.

One time when Mum and I were in Saint Andrews, we drove a few miles down the highway to St. Stephen, close to the Maine border. St. Stephen was a crumbling town with sooty, abandoned red-brick buildings and a gritty main street. We stopped at a drugstore to buy

Mum a new toothbrush and get some potato chips to have with our vermouth later, but the highlight of St. Stephen was Ganong's candy store. The Ganong chocolate factory was in a big brick building on the hill, and the company had its own store in town. I bought two packs of Ganong's famous Chicken Bones (pink, candy-covered chocolate) to take home to BC as gifts.

That night it snowed, a light dusting over Saint Andrews' cold, bare streets. There was ice on the Enforcer in the morning. On the way back to Fredericton we stopped in again at Steven's house. His brother was chopping and stacking wood in the driveway, and Steven had the fire going in his living room. He showed us all the pickles he had preserved while we were in Saint Andrews—two hundred jars!

I gave Mum her eye drops on Steven's pink velvet couch and poured some cherry-flavoured cough medicine into a spoon to soothe her irritated throat. Mum tilted her head back and opened her mouth. She couldn't see the spoon, so she pursed her lips, ready for my aim, and I poured the cough syrup into her mouth perfectly, just like a mother bird with a baby. Steven served us some corn chowder and pickles on his mother's china at the dining room table. He'd made rolls, too, and an apple pie.

CHAPTER EIGHT

O N A SUNNY, CRISP, SEPTEMBER day in 2013 I arrived in Fredericton to visit Mum and Dad, this time for a distressing reason. Dad had had surgery for throat cancer at the Fredericton hospital, and now he had decided to have radiation treatment, which had to be done in Saint John. Poor Dad. He had to have all his teeth pulled out in preparation; he'd had a lot of metal work done in his mouth throughout his life, and the doctors thought radiation would not be a good mix with that. I knew from Mum that Dad was being fed through a gruesome stomach tube in the hospital, but apparently he was alert and mobile, and he could leave the hospital in the afternoons as long as he was back for "dinner" (six syringes of vanilla Boost).

Dad had recently bought a big, ugly new car, a Venza, and Mum had the car keys waiting for me. I put my bag in the room where I stayed during my visits, which was actually Dad's office. He had his plants on the windowsill, and on the walls he'd hung some paintings and prints of fishing camps on the Miramichi River and a selection of photographs I had sent him over the years of my life out west. Art books filled the shelves, along with some chipped Inuit sculpture, a jar of Dad's paintbrushes, and a stack of journals that contained his accounts.

Ernie, Mum and Dad's cat, always greeted me by coming into my room, rubbing up against my leg, and then leaving. He was a funny old thing, a tabby with one white leg that stuck straight out sideways because it had been broken early in his life. Dad had got him from a woman in Oromocto who had allergies, the wife of a fisherman friend. Ernie loved Dad, and he slept on his bed with him at night.

Mum and I drove up to the hospital to visit Dad. I didn't know what to expect when I saw him, and I was nervous about driving his huge car up the hill and through the university. The car had a Ducks Unlimited sticker on the side window and a screen on the dashboard that showed the road behind you, so you could see if you were about to back into something.

When we got to the hospital, Dad was washing his hands in the sink off his room, calm and fully dressed.

"Hi, Dad," I greeted him. "Would you like to go home for the afternoon?"

He had to speak by holding a little tube in his throat. He didn't seem depressed or anything, just a little weaker. The three of us shuffled down the hallway past the nurses' station. Dad looked at the nurse behind the counter and said, with his rough, strained breath, "Don't wait up."

All the nurses loved Dad. "See you later, Bruno," they called as they waved.

Nurses amaze me. They seem to live life for the moment, and they're so steady—they go about their business as if it's all just routine. I wonder if they're ever thinking, "Hmmm, that man might be dead in a week . . ."

Dad asked for a wheelchair when we got to the elevator. Mum wandered on ahead while I went to find one. "Wait here," I said to Dad once he was seated. I had to pursue Mum, who had walked into a huge closet—quite unlike her. She and I were laughing as we headed back toward Dad, who had one of his exasperated smirks on his face.

He looked at Mum, then at me, and then pointed back at Mum and said, "It's time . . . it's time." It was a light moment, but long after that, when Mum remembered Dad, she'd say, "Do you remember what Bruno said? 'It's time . . . it's time.' Oh, this is no golden age."

I got both Mum and Dad loaded into the Venza, and we went back home and spent a nice afternoon there. Dad shuffled around with his plants and went through his mail, and Mum and I went for a walk along the river. Around tea time the house was full of Dad's friends—his neighbour Celvyn, his fishing pal Gary, his friend Shawn Graham from up the street who used to be the premier. They settled in with their beer or Scotch. Celvyn said, "Good crop of tomatoes you have out there, Bruno," and Dad said, "What I wouldn't give to have a bite of those."

When I brought Dad home from the hospital the next afternoon, he wanted to make apple jelly, and he wanted me to learn how he did it. He made masses every year of what he called "jelly juice" from wild apples that contained natural pectin. We got out the jelly juice and the sugar, the jars, and a lemon, and set to work. But Dad was exhausted in no time. He lay down on the couch, and I continued the work. I didn't really want to, but I felt sorry for him lying there with that plastic tube protruding from his thin neck. I kept going, stirring and bottling, and when I was finished I sat down to rest with Dad. He asked for a notepad and pen, and then he wrote out, in a weak and unsteady hand—such a different hand from the one he had had only a month earlier, when he had sketched poplars by the river at his fishing camp—a few directions, in case I ever wanted to make apple jelly again. It seemed like such a valiant thing to do when he was so ill. Of all the items I still have of Dad's, his little jelly-juice scrawl is my most treasured.

The next afternoon, I fetched Dad again. Celvyn, his wife, Beth, Mum, and I wanted to surprise Dad and take him in Celvyn's truck up to the fishing camp, the place where Dad was happiest. The camp was about a hundred miles north of Fredericton, up the river. Celvyn drove, but I could tell Dad was anxious; halfway there, as we crossed a small wooden bridge, Dad indicated that he wanted to go home. It had been a good effort, to try to take him to his beloved camp, but he just couldn't do it. Celvyn turned the truck around, and on the way home we stopped at his friend's home on the river. Celvyn's friend was out, but Dad shuffled across the big lawn to look down at the deep, brown water that was full of fish. At least he got to see the river, a place where he had felt so contented and at peace.

When we got home, Dad asked me to give him a haircut. He wanted one before he began the radiation treatments. Dad was mainly bald, but he felt that the back of his neck was scraggly. I did the best I could while Mum sat with a glass of wine in a stream of autumn sun that shone through the window, in between Dad's geraniums.

The doorbell rang, and it was the Meals on Wheels man with two dinners on round aluminum plates. Mum gave me a glance and whispered as I put them in the fridge, "I'd rather have soup, but Bruno insists on receiving these dinners. The guy who delivers them is older than us!"

After I had taken Dad back to the hospital, Mum and I heated up the meals and ate our sole, green beans, and mashed potatoes at the dining room table by candlelight. Mum flushed her calcium pills down the toilet before our little walk around the block under the moon, and then we had an early bedtime.

The next day, Dad went by ambulance to Saint John to begin his radiation treatments. Mum and I planned to drive down in a day or two to visit him. We walked along the river, and then I took Mum across town to have her hair cut at Headmasters Headmistress Hairstyling. Diane had cut Mum's hair for years, and Mum loved her—she was so steady, kind, and friendly. Diane came out to the parking lot and took Mum's arm, then gently washed her hair once we got inside and gave her a nice cut. Mum whispered to me as Diane helped her with her coat, "Anny, give dear Diane a big tip."

The day we drove to Saint John was gloriously clear and sunny, with a big blue sky and red and orange leaves fluttering in a warm autumn breeze. Along the scenic route beside the river, bushels of apples and piles of pumpkins were for sale at the farm stands, and cows grazed contentedly.

The Saint John hospital was gigantic, with a massive lobby that looked like the food court in a mall. Dad was in the cancer ward. I had picked a little bouquet for him from his garden—daisies, nasturtiums, and marigolds. He was sitting up in a chair, but he looked thin and tired in his blue hospital gown. He could barely hold up his head, and he indicated with his hand that I should give the flowers to the nurses. It was difficult to see him like that. All I could think of was to tell him that Ernie said hello. Mum sat across from Dad in a turquoise vinyl chair. Her feet hurt, so I found a footstool for her.

Mum asked, "Are you in pain, Bruno?"

Dad slowly shook his head, then said, in his weary, breathless way, holding the tube in his neck and looking at the bottom of Mum's shoes, "Molly, get your soles fixed."

Out in the hall, Mum pulled a worn tissue from her pocket and had a quiet cry. "That's it," she said. "He'll not get out of this." A kind nurse came over and led us to a small room where there was tea and a big soft black couch. Mum didn't cry on my shoulder; she just bent forward a little, wiping her eyes. It's quite an empty feeling to see and hear your mother cry. The only other time I heard her sobbing was the night Gran died.

After a while I said to Mum, "Let's go out in the sun and go somewhere, a country drive or something."

Mum said through her tears, "Not yet. I just want to sit for a little while longer."

Then a beautiful, dark young woman came into the room and sat down across from us. "I'm Amanda," she said. "Bruno's doctor." She paused for a moment.

"It's okay," I said. "Mum and I can handle it."

"Bruno and I have talked," Amanda said, "and I've grown to really like him." She was so gentle, which I suppose doctors need to be, as she continued, "I prefer to keep him here in Saint John rather than risk him getting injured in the ambulance going back to Fredericton. He's so weak." Then she said that if it was okay with us ("the family"), she would stop Dad's fluids, or something like that. Mum and I were a little stunned at the whole situation. Amanda assured us that Dad was comfortable and not in pain. She didn't say "I'm sorry" or "I feel your loss" or any other cliché, which I found refreshing.

Eventually, Mum and I walked out into the bright sun and got into the Venza. Mum had a good friend named Mary Blatherwick who lived about forty miles down the road on the Kennebecasis River, just east of Saint John. Mary had invited us for lunch if we were in the area, so we set off and found her house easily. Mary was down on the dock with her husband when we arrived, tying up a canoe, so Mum and I sat on the steps in the sun, feeling a little depressed. Then I remembered that there was a bottle of vermouth in the car. I got it for Mum, who took a few gulps from the bottle because we didn't have any glasses. Mary served us chicken soup in her sunny kitchen, and a calico cat named Phoebe sat on Mum's lap and purred. I think that gave Mum great comfort, stroking the little cat.

We decided to take a new route back to Fredericton—two cable ferries over the river and across two islands. It was lovely, driving slowly along the sparkling river past meadows and farmhouses. When we got home, we had a little toast to Dad. Beth stopped by, and we shared our fondest memories and funniest stories about Dad.

Mum said, "Can you believe he told me to get my soles fixed?" and we had a big laugh. "Poor Bruno," she said.

Early the next morning it was raw and grey outside. While Mum was having her tea in her big old stuffed chair and I was drinking my coffee on Dad's fake-leather couch, we got the call that Dad had died in the night. Mum and I sat in the living room for hours, not saying much. Every so often she'd murmur, looking out the window at the wilting garden and dead yellow leaves, "Gosh, I can't believe he's gone." I didn't change out of my pyjamas until noon, when people started arriving with pies and pots of chili. I put everything in the freezer in the basement.

Mum was stoic and very strong. By mid-afternoon we were ready to get some air, so I took her arm and we ambled along the river down to the railway bridge. Mum wore her Belarussian boots, and I wore Dad's green raincoat. "He had a good life, considering his sad beginnings," Mum said.

"A very successful life," I added. "And just think of the hundreds of times he stood in the river fishing, or smoked fish in his smokehouse, or gardened and puttered around."

I flew back to Victoria a few days later, but over the weeks that followed, I received reports from family friends in Fredericton that Mum was alone and sad in the house. Winter had arrived by then. The sidewalks were icy, the trees bare, the river frozen, and the sunlight brief. Mum told me on the phone that she spent most of her time lying in bed listening to the radio.

One day when I called her, though, she sounded cheerier. "I'm finished grieving now," she said, and then, just like that, "I've decided to go to a home." As a war artist, Mum had been a uniformed officer in the Canadian army during the Second World War, so she was eligible to move into the veterans' facility up the hill next to the hospital.

I was shocked. I couldn't imagine Mum in a home, especially with all those old male veterans, some of whom I was sure would shriek in the night. (It turned out I was right. One elderly fellow used to yell, "Look out!" from his wheelchair in the hallway, sending Mum and me into gales of laughter.) My initial reaction was a combination of melancholy, relief, and slight disappointment. Melancholy seems to sink into me whenever I, or someone around me, is vulnerable. I was a bit relieved, because I knew Mum was feeling she couldn't take care of herself anymore, but I was disappointed that she had capitulated to an institution. "An old folks' home—a nursing home," I kept saying to myself. It seemed like only yesterday that Mum was digging worms for my chickens and painting her vivid crowd scenes of the Fredericton Exhibition or a parade on Queen Street.

Over the past few months, I had asked Mum on many occasions if she'd like to move out west with me. She wanted to remain in Fredericton, she said. She loved her friends and her life there. But she had barely been out since Dad died, except to go to dinner next door at Beth's or to Heather and Anne's on the other side. Her friend Mary Blatherwick dropped by often, but the bitter winter weather and biting winds made it almost impossible for Mum to go for walks or enjoy the fresh air.

I flew back to help her move. The flight across Canada was smooth the entire way, and the sun glinted off the airplane's wings all the way from the Rockies to the Fredericton tarmac. Heather brought Mum out to the airport to pick me up. She was bundled up in a new duffle coat Heather and Anne had bought her in Maine, along with her llama hat and Cowichan mittens.

The arrivals area in Fredericton has large windows, so you can see the crowd of anxious people waiting to greet the passengers. Mum was usually standing by the window—I would spot her quickly, because of her white hair, and Dad would be standing back beside the Trius Taxi sign and the car rental booth. This time, Heather was the one waiting in the crowd, calm and smiling. Mum was sitting on the red plastic seats beside the luggage carrousel, wringing her mittened hands together with excitement. Gran used to do the same thing. When Mum and I walked off the ferry from Vancouver to Galiano Island, me carrying the trolls, Gran was always on the dock, dressed in her blue Simpsons-Sears smock, wringing her hands in wonderful anticipation of our visit.

It was a happy reunion. Heather drove us back to Mum's house. After a glass of wine, I made a soup from some fish Dad had caught and frozen the summer before, adding some of the dill he had dried and stored in a can above the stove. I watered Dad's dry geraniums and the other cuttings he had planted in his homemade clay pots on the windowsill.

Dad had rigged up a bird feeder the squirrels couldn't figure out, a pole with a garbage can lid around it. Mum had managed to keep it filled after he died, struggling outside with a bucket full of sunflower seeds and making her way down the frozen steps. She'd always worried about the birds during Fredericton's cruel winters, and sometimes she'd bought bacon just for them. One mourning dove had taken a liking to Dad, sitting in the garden as he scratched the soil and nurtured his plants. The dove even sat on Dad's arm when he rested on the bench under the apple tree. I thought quite a lot about that little dove after Dad died, knowing she would miss him.

The house was clean, thanks to Mum's housecleaner, Cora. Cora lived in a village on the other side of the river; she weighed about eighty pounds soaking wet, but she was strong and wiry and a hard worker. Mum and Cora adored each other, and now that Mum was left alone in the house, Cora often dropped in after a day of housecleaning somewhere else to bring Mum some soup or just to sit and keep her company. I suspected that Mum had cried on Cora's shoulder once or twice—they had a very strong connection.

Mum and I sat and drank wine as the soup simmered. When it got dark, I turned on some lamps, which gave a nice glow to the tiled floors and the oil paintings on the wall in the quiet house. Mum told me that Dad's fishing pals had sprinkled his ashes in the river at the fishing camp. They had even made him a brass plaque and installed it on the riverbank.

It was a clear, starry night, with crusty snowbanks on the street corners. Mum and I walked to the end of Kensington Court and back, just far enough to get some cold air into our lungs. When we got back, we slurped our soup, watching reruns of *Fawlty Towers*. It was an enjoyable evening, but in the back of my mind was Mum's impending move to the Veterans Health Unit.

Over the next few weeks, Mum and I had a lovely time. I'd drive her up to Odell Park, where we'd amble around the frozen pond and under the bare trees, or she'd lie on the couch in the living room and I'd play Elgar or read aloud to her, or she'd doze while I made strange concoctions from obscure items in the downstairs freezer. As I was cleaning out the cupboards, Mum glanced up from her chair by the window and called, "Give all those stale Bugles and orange chips to the birds!"

Sometimes we looked through old photos from Mum's childhood, which she kept in a tattered album. Heather and Anne and their old dog, Sophie, came in for tea after work. Cora dropped by with muffins, and one afternoon Steven came for a visit; he was in town from Harvey to do errands. One evening while we were having a glass of wine with Beth, Mum was humming the old Peggy Lee song "Is That All There Is?" Beth looked up the lyrics on her iPhone, and we were all surprised at how gloomy they were—something about a house burning down and losing everything, so "let's break out the booze and have a ball."

One entertaining activity was sorting through a stack of art Dad had stored in the attic: prints, pastels, drawings, and etchings. As we thumbed through them slowly, leaning over the dining room table, Mum would say, "That was from our balcony in Norway," or "That was along the Thames." Mum also showed me a basket of the letters I had written to her since the day I left home—she'd kept them all. There were also some stories I had written and illustrated about the trolls—how the trolls had become hippies and how they drank beer, chewed grape bubble gum, said, "Hey, man," often, and watched the television show *Get Smart*. There was even a crayon drawing I had done when I was seven of a neighbour child's mother. The mother was not very friendly, so I had drawn her naked with a lot of hair and swirled breasts.

I had left home at seventeen, boarding a train bound for Vancouver. I was heading out west to a place I knew well. I had spent part of every summer as a kid on Galiano Island with Gran, and over the years I'd often stayed in West Vancouver with my godparents, Ted and Barbara Henderson. Barbara was Mum's best childhood friend. She and Ted lived in a house on Roseberry Avenue that had a wonderful view of the sea, Stanley Park, and the tall buildings in Vancouver's downtown. I'll never forget the smell of their house—cedar! Coming from the east, I found the aroma of the west coast enticing. Barbara and Ted's neighbour had a monkey puzzle tree, which always filled me with awe. To me, the west was pure magic, almost like a fantasy world. Behind Barbara and Ted's house was a wooded area, a rainforest with great hemlocks and yews and wild rhododendrons. The trolls made a secret fort there in an old rotting stump.

Barbara and Ted had three children, all slightly older than me: Scott, Jane, and Lesley. On their front lawn one sunny afternoon, I held a tea party for the trolls and brought out Lesley's bears and dolls to join us—Barbara had given me a little tea set from Chinatown. We sat on a blanket under a tree, waiting excitedly for Les to come home from school. The trolls had prepared tea, and Barbara had brought out a plate of refreshments. But when Les got home, she was aghast at finding all her bears and dollies on the lawn—I had taken them out of her room. She stormed past us and burst into tears in the kitchen, where Barbara scolded her for not being more generous. I've felt so guilty ever since!

Some summers, Ted and Barbara packed us all up and took us to their summer house in Kye Bay, a delightful spot on Vancouver Island. Kye Bay's sandbar stretched for miles when the tide went out, and we dug clams. Ted taught me to swim there by putting me on his back, and I remember his skin being soft and smooth and tanned, with hundreds of freckles across his shoulders, as I wrapped my arms around his neck. When I looked down through the clear water, I saw a million colours: blooming sea anemones, starfish, seaweeds, corals, and luminescent shells. Scott, Jane, and Les still have the summer cottage; I visit them there, and we still dig for clams.

I headed west the day I graduated from high school. I didn't wait for the prom—I didn't have any close friends or fabulous memories of school. Mum and Dad drove me out to Fredericton Junction at dusk, and we waited on the platform with two other people in silence. It must have been strange for them to see their second child leaving home. Dad said, "Remember, never borrow money," and Mum said, "Remember, you can always come home."

When the train arrived, I stepped up into the carriage. A conductor took my bag, and then he made me a bed in the lower berth by folding down the seats. I sat on the bed looking out at the darkness and eating an egg sandwich Mum had made for me—as usual, the bread fell apart, and the filling dripped onto the sheets. The train rolled on through the night, occasionally stopping at country towns and blowing its whistle when we crossed remote roads in the wilderness. Finally, I fell asleep.

I got a job at the Arts Club Theatre in Vancouver and found a tiny apartment in the West End. Every time Mum came out to visit me, we'd stroll down Granville Street. Whenever we passed the Hudson's Bay store, she'd say, "Mum and I always had a meat pie in the café at the Bay after we shopped." Every time we walked by the Hotel Vancouver on Georgia Street, Mum would point to it and say, "That's where I signed up for the army."

The hotel building had been used to house new recruits, and Mum often told the story of her first day in the army after signing up. Once she was given her uniform and assigned a bunk, she was immediately homesick and full of regret. When Gran came to see her, Mum begged Gran to take her home. Gran was very sympathetic. "I'll get you out!" she promised Mum. "I'll call Mackenzie King!" But after a few more days, Mum said, you couldn't have dragged her out of there. She loved the other girls, there was lots of food, and the drills were fun. After a while, she was sent for basic training in Edmonton.

While we were cleaning out her house in Fredericton, Mum gave me her wool army jacket, small and heavy, with a few badges sewn on the upper sleeve. She sang me a funny song she and her army girlfriends had made up in their barracks. It was sung to the tune of a march popular at the time, she said, and they'd bellow it out as they marched around the parade square:

> HITLER! The CWACs are on their way!
> HITLER, expect us any day,
> Good girls—we've cut off our curls,
> And the Nazis, the blighters, will PAY!
> Da da da-da da da da . . .

"What a time the war was," Mum recalled. "Of course, I went over toward the end, but I still saw horrid things. My worst memory is not actually the bombs or the fighting, but something I saw in Holland after the war ended. This manic blond Dutchman was pedalling his bicycle at a tremendous speed along a river. He had a rope in one hand, and it was tied to a German, who was running to keep up, like a dog being pulled. The German looked shocked and about to fall. It was tragic and awful, just the look of desperation on both men, although they were in such opposite circumstances."

In the attic, Mum found a little oil painting she had done when she was very young and living with her family on the farm in Vancouver. "That was my first oil painting of our garden," she told me. It was lovely: green shrubs of various tones and hues, one flowering pink tree, a winding grey path, and two people looking up at something in a white bush. Mum also gave me an oil painting called *Meal Parade*, which she had entered in the competition the Canadian government held in 1943 to see who would become the country's war artists. Mum's painting showed a group of women soldiers lined up outside waiting for dinner. It was nighttime, with the heavy-coated figures standing under a bare tree against a dark sky.

Mum and I often talked about the other Canadian war artists who had been sent overseas. One of my favourites was Goodridge Roberts, and Mum gave me a beautifully simple watercolour Goodridge had done called *Blue Sky and Clouds*. E.J. Hughes was an artist Mum loved. He painted brilliantly coloured scenes of west coast life—the sea and the forests, wharves, tugs, steamers, and other vessels, coastal fishing villages. Those were the paintings Hughes was most famous for, but he was also a war artist. Mum's favourite piece of war art, though, was from the First World War, a painting titled *For What?* by Fred Varley. The very title makes you weep. On a war-torn field under a pale yellow sky sits a cart full of dead soldiers.

There was a bit of a scandal involving Fred Varley and Harold Mortimer-Lamb, Mum's father. At one point, Varley's model, Vera Weatherbie, became his lover. Varley had a large family, and the situation was apparently upsetting to all concerned. Eventually, however, Vera ended up with Harold. They married, with Gran's encouragement, and had a long and happy marriage. Harold and Vera lived in a lovely home full of art and jade sculptures up on Burnaby Mountain, with a spectacular view out toward Vancouver. Their terraced garden on the hill had a goldfish pond, and I would float the trolls on the lily pads while Mum visited her father and Vera. Vera and Harold had an old chocolate Labrador too, named Abby. Vera was thin and nervous, very elegant in her woollen dresses and silver bracelets, with her hair caught up in a bun.

Mum told me that when she was a girl, her father didn't pay much attention to her and her half-brothers, to the house, or to Gran. "He'd eat alone in his study every night," said Mum. Sometimes on Sundays, when he golfed, he'd take Mum to caddy for him, "and then he'd buy me an orange soda," she recalled. Overall, I don't think Harold was a family man—Mum said he was aloof. He was happiest alone with Vera, surrounded by his art.

Harold died in his sleep at the age of ninety-nine. On the last visit I made with Mum to see him, he was sitting in bed, propped up by what looked like a thousand down pillows, wizened and frail, with a wispy white beard and very pink skin. He held out a trembling arm toward me. I was terrified; I hardly knew him and was not a touching type of child anyway, not very affectionate with anyone except my animals and the trolls. However, I bent forward, and Harold weakly embraced me. He smelled of fresh soap, I remember.

Vera stayed on alone in the house. After I moved to Vancouver, I used to take the bus from my apartment on English Bay all the way up Burnaby Mountain to see her. Vera became more and more high-strung over the few years I knew her. She suffered from some sort of mental disorder toward the end of her life—she'd tell me that Tommy Douglas was hiding in the fridge.

When Vera died, Mum came out to deal with the estate, and I met her long-lost half-brother Hal, who was big, had a protruding lower lip, and smelled of whisky. I was allowed to select two things from the house, so I chose a down duvet and six plates with roses on them. I used that duvet for thirty-five years, until I forgot to bring it in from the pig barn on the farm one night and Matilda, my eight-hundred-pound sow, gave birth to twelve piglets on it. I had been sleeping in the barn to keep an eye on Matilda's sister, Mabel, who had gastric condition. I still have two of the rose-patterned plates.

There was a sad story Mum told me, when she was visiting me out west, about Vera and her father. Mum had decided to visit her father one evening in 1942. She went up to Burnaby Mountain and found the house locked, so she crawled in a window and ran into Vera and Harold. All three of them were shocked for a moment. Then her father said,

"Moll, I was married today." Vera straightened her dress and said in her nervous voice, "To me. Do you mind?"

Mum told me that she did indeed mind, that she was terribly hurt, but she never said anything more about the incident. I don't know who I felt for most when I heard the story, Vera or Mum. Both women were, at that moment, very vulnerable, surprised by each other, and Mum must have felt that her father had abandoned her and had a moment of complete aloneness, even emptiness. It's a horrid feeling when you realize you are alone in the universe. I have experienced it a few times in my adult life. It comes on quite unexpectedly, a deep, almost primitive understanding that you are alone, despite the people around you.

Mum went happily to bed after our long days of reminiscing, sorting, chatting, napping, and walking. I'd set up a bed for her downstairs, because she had twice fallen down the stairs in the night, tripping over Ernie to let him out. She ended up covered in bruises but never broke a bone. Mum thought it was hilarious, taking these tumbles, but they scared me. Once Mum was asleep, I quietly sorted through her clothing, packing a selection of nice clothes in a battered grey suitcase Mum and Dad had bought in 1960. It had been in the closet for years, since Mum always preferred her tattered blue nylon bag.

The veterans' place had given Mum a yellow plastic binder containing information about what to pack and other things. I skimmed over the part about helping your parents cope with the change, but I noticed there was absolutely NO LATEX OR LOBSTER permitted in the facility due to staff allergies. No balloons, then? All clothing was to be labelled with the resident's name.

"Just like camp," I joked to Mum, trying to ease our looming stress.

"Just like the army," she said.

The day before her move, Mum and I took a drive around the Plats, with its quiet, treed streets and old Loyalist homes. When we got back to the house, Mum prepared for her usual bath before dinner. "I have to be clean for the Barracks," she said lightly, in a feeble voice. I ran her a bath downstairs and was watching the news when I heard her call me. "Anny, can you help me? I can't get out of the tub."

I suddenly realized just how old Mum was. She'd been able to have a bath on her own all her life. Not being able to get out of the tub was worse than falling down the stairs. Anybody could fall down the stairs in the dark, but getting stuck in the bathtub was alarming. I had never thought of Mum as weak, really, and this meant she was almost helpless. I helped her by lifting her out from behind, holding her under her thin arms. Normally, we would have had a laugh at our human frailties and clumsiness, but that night we didn't. I wonder if Mum was thinking the same thing I was, that our roles had reversed for real this time.

The next morning was still and grey, a dull winter's day. The sand truck had come along in the night, so the streets were gritty, and the snow shoved to the sides was a crusty brown. The plan was to take Mum up to the veterans' facility in the afternoon, but first she had to go to the hospital for some tests and other health checks.

I planned to settle Mum in her room, unpack her bag, have dinner with her there, and then come back to the house, tidy up, and go to bed early. Beth had kindly offered to take Ernie, so I would head over to her place at the crack of dawn, we decided, visit Mum for breakfast in the facility, and then catch my plane home.

I made Mum her tea that morning, and then we did her eye drops. We were both so quiet we could hear the clock ticking. Neither of us could eat anything. Mum threw her calcium pills down the toilet as usual, and then I packed a few toiletries in a cotton pouch she'd had for years—her toothbrush, comb, Nivea cream, and Yardley's rose powder.

We sat in the living room until it was time to go. Mum said, "Am I really going to a home?" and I said, "Yes, but if you don't like it, remember, you can leave. You can come back to the house and we can hire a girl." (I didn't say "caregiver" on purpose.)

"No," Mum said, and then in a sad, little voice she added, "I don't think I can look after myself, and a girl is such an intrusion." I think we both felt as if we were waiting for the executioner.

I kept getting up to do trivial things such as checking the thermostat and washing our teacups, or making bland comments about how there used to be much more snow and bluer winter skies when we'd lived on Grey Street forty-five years earlier.

"Yes," Mum said. "Remember how you'd ski like a bat out of hell down those mountains?"

I fell into a sort of trance from the waiting. Everything became detailed and exaggerated, just like it had the time I was locked in that room in Belarus and I'd started to count the rings on a broken plastic-covered table to stay focused. The clock ticking above the kitchen sink got louder. Dad's ceramic-tile coffee table felt colder to the touch, and I noticed there was dirt lodged between the tiles that had probably been there for years. Ernie's cat hair clung to a Moroccan blanket that hung over the back of a chair frayed at the edges from past pets clawing at it. A book of poems by Alden Nowlan, a New Brunswick poet, had a tea stain on its mauve cover, I could see, and a delicate cobweb was strung between a geranium and the blue curtains.

I was clammy but not cold, anxious but calm, in a trance but alert. I don't know what I was. Finally, I could bear it no more, and I suggested a walk around the block. I had to help Mum get her boots on and do up her coat, and then we walked slowly down the street in the still air, arm in arm as usual. Everything seemed to be in black and white. The only colour came from the sand speckled over what snow was left on the roadside.

We were due at the hospital in mid-morning. I helped Mum into the car and put her suitcase in the back seat. We drove up the hill and through the university. "I designed those stained-glass windows," Mum said as we passed a building called Memorial Hall.

Mum was on file in the computer at the hospital when we reported in, and things went smoothly. First she had her heart checked: a technician hooked her up to a machine full of wires that measured its rhythm. Mum did just as she was told—"Lie still, breathe normally, this may be cold, but it won't hurt." Then it was off for a chest X-ray on the other side of the building. As we made our way like zombies through the dim hallways, we passed a woman on a gurney. She was groaning as she lay under a single sheet, all alone. I'll never forget it, though I don't think Mum noticed.

Mum had to strip naked for the X-ray and then put on a gown. I helped her with it in the tiny, curtained booth. When the nurse said, "Turn to your left," Mum didn't move, so I gently pushed her sideways, and so it continued: "Turn right"; "Left arm up"; "Right arm up." The only thing Mum could do on her own was "Look forward; face front now."

It was dusk by the time the hospital tests were concluded. It was a relief to get outdoors, even though we were in a massive parking lot covered in sand and salt. As we crossed the dirty pavement toward the Venza, Mum asked, "Can we go home now?" I had to remind her that we were only going next door, to the veterans' home, but that I'd brought vermouth and wine, which were allowed, and she could have a drink in her new room, and then dinner there, and then she could go to bed. "Will you be with me?" Mum asked. I said that I'd stay for dinner, but then I had to go back to the house and feed Ernie. "Ernie's a lucky old cat," Mum said. "He never liked me anyway. He liked Bruno."

We drove over to the veterans' place. We had to buzz to get in. "In case we're terrorists," I said to Mum, trying to make a joke. We were pitiful as we staggered in arm in arm, me carrying a suitcase in one hand. A nurse told us that Mum's room was number eleven, down the hall to the left. "Am I really in a home?" Mum whispered as we moved along past carts of laundry and medicines, and rooms with old men on reclining beds watching television. Dinner had already been served, at four o'clock, so there was a lingering aroma of cooked food in the hallways.

We found room eleven, a freshly painted room with a bed, a lamp, a chair, and a private bathroom. There was no bathtub, though—baths were given in a room down the hall once a week or when requested. I noticed on her chart that Mum's bath time was Friday night. She had a large window that looked out on Regent Street, the main street that led up to the malls.

I sat Mum down and then unpacked her things, including her two antique Italian goblets. "Look, Old Pup," I said. "I brought wine and glasses! Let's have a drink." The drink helped a little bit.

Mum said, "I'm shaking," and then, in a small voice, "I hope I make some friends here."

As Mum sat on the edge of her bed, lonely and nervous, I suddenly saw myself, years earlier, sitting on the edge of a cot in a "girls' school" (that's what Mum called it) in England. Mum and Dad had gone off to France for the summer months to paint, and I was alone and frightened.

A gentle nurse soon arrived in Mum's room. "You must be Molly—welcome," she said. "Would you like dinner?"

"We'd love it," I said. "It's been a stressful day."

Mum and I were seated at a round table in the home's dining area, just the two of us. Our server gave Mum a bib, but I quickly whipped it aside. We had a plastic glass of cranberry juice, then some pork in orange sauce, mashed potatoes, cooked carrots, and peas. There was a time in my life when I had longed to eat a routine dinner like this with my parents every night. I'd usually eaten cereal alone in my room with the trolls, by choice, but underneath I craved a routine. Whenever I stayed with Gran on Galiano Island, she would cook a roast on Saturdays, served with peas, and we'd sit and watch *Hockey Night in Canada* while we ate—she was a fan. Then she'd put me to bed in cool cotton sheets and read me Grimm's *Fairy Tales*—the more gruesome the better! When I was older, I stayed for a while with Uncle Abby, Mum's half-brother, and his wife, Irene, in England. They drank sherry at the same time every Sunday afternoon while they read the weekly papers, then took a walk through the country lanes, passing the stone church where Abby was the minister. Having a normal dinner at the veterans' facility that first evening was comforting, at least for me.

The dessert tray, served after the main course, was amazing. "I feel as if I'm in the Empress Hotel!" I said to Mum. There was a selection of puddings, cakes, pastries, ice creams, pies, fruits, and custards. And then coffee or tea. "Just like the Ritz," I said to Mum to cheer her.

She muttered, "Not quite."

"Remember how they left a chocolate on our pillow every night?" I persisted.

Mum and I had stayed at the Ritz-Carlton when we'd gone to Montreal to launch a children's book we'd done together—*The True Tale of Merlin the Billy Dog*. It was about a few of the funny animals on my farm, specifically the friendship that had formed between the smelly old goat, Merlin, and my portly black Labrador, Alice-Mary. I wrote the text for the book and Mum did the illustrations. It was handmade, printed on beautiful paper created by two women in Sidney, BC, who owned an antique printing press. Mum and I called them "the apple ladies," because they also pressed the apples from their orchard and made cider.

Mum and I had a wonderful time in Montreal. Not only was there the book launch, but Mum caught up with old friends. One of them, whom she loved dearly, was Tom Tebbutt, who wrote about tennis for the *Globe and Mail*. Tom had once invited Mum to the tennis matches at Wimbledon and at Roland Garros in Paris to paint them. Her big oil paintings of matches on the green grass courts of England and the rust-coloured clay of France, with all the crowds and the little white figures on the court, were very popular.

After our fine dining at the veterans' facility, I thought it would be a good idea for Mum to lie down, even though it was still only seven. I turned on her radio, setting it to the CBC, and helped her change into her flannelette nightie. I told her I'd be back first thing in the morning for breakfast before I caught my flight, and then I'd return in a month or so and we'd go off on a road trip. In the meantime, I said, she had nothing to worry about. Heather and Anne would have her over for dinner, friends would visit her in her room ("There's wine and vermouth in your cupboard," I reminded her), and Ernie would have a grand home with Beth. The house was well built and would sell quickly. But I might as well have been talking to the wall, since Mum was in a daze, totally exhausted. When I got back outside to the parking lot, the temperature had dipped considerably. The Venza's tires squeaked on the snow as I backed out.

The silent house, though warm, felt very empty. I switched on the hall light, and there was Ernie, sitting at the top of the stairs.

He hobbled down with his stiff leg, and I gave him some kibble at his place near the breadbox Dad had carved years ago. As I was packing my bag, I went through Dad's closet and took a couple of sweaters and his Order of Canada pin. (When I got home to Victoria, I discovered his sweaters were full of holes, so I used them as cat beds instead.) I packed a glass paperweight I had made for Dad when I took a glass-blowing course one time; he had always kept it beside his bed. I took a few of the books Mum and I had read together: *Great Tales from English History* (our favourite), *The Moonstone*, by Wilkie Collins, *Intimate Letters of English Kings*, and one of Mum's favourite novels, *A Passage to India*, by E.M. Forster. Finally, I packed Gran's old white cream jug.

Feeling a little sentimental, I decided to have a martini, which I made with the last drop of vodka in Dad's cabinet and a stale olive I found in the fridge. Mum and Dad hated sentimentality, especially in their paintings, but there I was, on a freezing winter's night, sitting with old Ernie on Dad's bed as he waited for Dad to come home—he still did that every night. I felt I was entitled to pretend I was in a movie, to raise my glass to the empty house and ask, "What is life about?"

I woke up very early the next morning. Ernie was sleeping in my open suitcase. I puttered around the house, packing up a bag of food for Beth. I made coffee, then sat in Mum's chair in the living room and looked out the window. Fresh snow rested on the branches of the great, bare elms in the amber glow of the street light. The ground was pure white. I carried three litter boxes over to Beth's porch, then the bag of food and my luggage. Beth had offered to take me to the airport after we checked on Mum.

At six o'clock in the morning, I loaded Ernie into a carrier Heather had loaned me. Even though Beth lived so close by, our plan was that I would carry Ernie over and we would put him in Beth's basement until he settled in at her house. I put one of Dad's old T-shirts in the carrier so Ernie would have Dad's scent with him. I turned off the porch light and locked the door, then carried Ernie down the snowy brick steps. It was still dark, but dawn was beginning to appear above the roofs and chimneys. I trudged along on the crisp snow in the biting cold, and Ernie started to howl. I thought, I am truly leaving the neighbourhood—an era has passed. Goodbye, house.

My years of visiting Mum and Dad here, surrounded by their paintings, their books, and the old furniture Dad had restored, with birds clustered around the feeder outside, soup simmering on the stove, and hours and hours of British comedies to entertain us, had come to a close.

CHAPTER NINE

MUM MADE A REAL EFFORT to adjust to her new life at the Veterans Health Unit, though the first few weeks were difficult. I was relieved that she was safe, no longer in danger of falling down the stairs, or getting stuck in the bath, or setting the house on fire, which she had done once by trying to light a bunch of scrap paper in the oil stove when Dad was away fishing—she'd forgotten it was not a wood stove. She'd laughed her head off when she told me the story. "The house was full of smoke. I called 911, and the charming firemen arrived in their big yellow suits, such gentlemen, lumbering around with their extinguishers, asking if I needed oxygen. Bruno, of course, had a fit and said that was the reason his lemon verbena died." Ernie was apparently thriving at Beth's. Beth said he loved to sit on the kitchen table as Celvyn oiled his fishing reels and sorted out his tackle box. Ernie even bullied Millie, their little dog, for a place on Beth's bed.

I phoned Mum every two or three days and sent long letters with photographs enclosed once a week. After a couple of months, I could tell that she was happier. On the phone she'd say, "I'm going out tonight to Heather and Anne's," or "Mary and I walked along the river yesterday." One day she was very excited. "You'll never guess who came to see

me," she said. "That sweet, intelligent Eleanor Wachtel from the CBC."
Another day she said, "You'll never guess who I received a postcard
from—Tom Tebbutt! 'Hugs from Down Under,' it said."

She loved most of the nurses too. "They take me for a bath," Mum
told me, "and the water is so warm, and then they wrap me in a thick
towel and take me down to dinner—oh, it's heaven."

I'd pass along the news from Victoria: "Well, there's a little light
rain, but it's mild"; "The bulbs have begun to poke through the grass";
"I'm taking Archie to the beach soon—the tide is out." Or "I think I'll
do the first mow of the year—it's a beautiful day." Mum would say, "Oh,
you lucky people out there in the land of the daffodils. I'm looking out,
and all I see is brown ice and black trees."

When I made trips to Fredericton to visit Mum, I usually rented a
car at the airport so we could be independent. The days of the Impaler
and the Enforcer were over; the car I got was small, computerized,
and modern, something called a Probe. "What a revolting name for a
car," Mum said, quite rightly. The Probe had a weird-looking key and
door latches so sleek that half the time Mum and I couldn't see them.
Sometimes we took the Probe out to Steven's camp or down to the
Hilton in Saint John for a night. However, most of our time was spent
dozing and chatting in Mum's room, visiting her friends, and taking
short walks in various parks or along the river.

Mum was much weaker by then, because she spent so much time
napping on her bed. The nurses offered to take her for walks around
the place, but Mum didn't want to put them to the trouble. I think Mum
was simply tired and liked lying under Judy's purple quilt, listening
to the CBC. The Legion ladies in their white skirts and blue blazers
brought around chocolate bars once a week. Mum never ate them, so
I'd take a pile of them home to Victoria in my luggage—three Coffee
Crisps, two Kit Kats, four Oh Henry!s. The nurses at the facility always
brought me a cot that they put beside Mum's bed, and sometimes Mum
and I would talk and chuckle late into the night.

I worried that Mum might bring up subjects I couldn't bear, or things
that would embarrass me, but she never did. Every so often I would

let a personal comment slip, especially after a glass or two of wine. I said once, "I wonder what it feels like to be successful," and Mum lay there and replied, "Don't be silly—you are successful."

"Well, I don't feel successful," I said. "I wonder what it is like to *feel* successful, to be confident."

Mum said, "Like who?" and I don't why, but I blurted out, "Like Ann-Marie MacDonald." I regretted saying it as soon as it came out of my mouth, but by then it was too late. "She's so cool and successful," I went on, "and thin, and I bet she never makes a mistake, ever!"

Mum was silent for a moment, and then she said, "Well, she seems very disciplined."

Mum and I also talked about the travels we had taken over the years, together and apart. I had once gone on a river cruise from Moscow to Saint Petersburg with my friend Patsy. Patsy was married to a man who was fairly conservative and feared communism, but Patsy was a bit of a radical. When her husband died, I persuaded her to come on the Russian cruise with me, and we had a wonderful time. We spent much of our time on the bridge, smoking cheap Russian cigars and watching the Russian sun go down. We also entered the vodka shot competition, which I won. The vodka must have been watered down, because I had eight shots and Patsy had six, and we both were stone sober. The other guests looked at us with disdain after that, but we didn't care. A musical group from Moscow sang folk songs in the lounge, three burly men in beards and puff-sleeved blouses, and a bedraggled woman with a husky voice in a loose peasant skirt. Patsy and I were usually the only people up there.

It was an austere and dazzling trip, like the Russians themselves, sensitive but rough. Perhaps that's what lies at the heart of true art, what it means to be truly human—our weaknesses and our greatnesses are both within us. When you see them at the same time, it's very moving.

Patsy was a great friend, and we had many adventures together. She died of cancer a few years ago, which was very sad. She spent her last weeks at home, looking out to sea through her window while lying in a special hospital bed they had brought in, wearing a woollen cap.

I took her some quince branches with delicate red flowers that were just about to open. "Patsy, didn't we have fun!" I said. "Remember smoking on that Russian ship in the fog!" She held my hand weakly and cried.

Mum had always wanted to visit Russia and the Eastern Bloc countries, but she never did. She spent many winters in Spain, though, on little islands where she and Dad would sketch and pick oranges and sip red vermouth. I heard hilarious snippets about her travels over the years. One time when she was in France, she was wearing a new pair of contact lenses. She was one of the first people to wear contacts, and one of them fell into the bowl of pea soup she was eating. "The French were appalled when I put my fingers in the soup," she'd told me, laughing, "but I found it!"

All the nurses and the social workers liked Mum, because she was lucid and funny and interesting to talk to. Mum was often in the Fredericton paper, the *Daily Gleaner*, as a local celebrity and war veteran, or because she had given money to some charity or donated art to something. After Dad died, Mum and I had decided we should auction off some of his art collection for charity. We agreed the exhibit should be at Gallery 78, which was owned by a close friend of Mum's, Inge Pataki. Inge's daughter, Germaine, had taken over the running of the gallery because Inge had gone blind, but Inge still had a wonderful presence, and she attended every gallery opening. Some pieces in the exhibit were by Mum and Dad, but there were works by other local artists too. It turned out to be a grand affair.

Mum and I were excited—gallery openings are always great fun. I had packed a colourful cotton skirt for Mum to take with her to the veterans' facility in case she ever needed to dress up, and here was the occasion. The skirt was made by a company in the Maritimes called Suttles & Seawinds, but Mum kept calling it, by a slip of the tongue, "sea farts and scuttles," and we started laughing so hard I couldn't get her skirt buttoned. She even fell backwards on her bed, she was laughing so much, and between hoots I said, "Old Pup, please sit upright so that I may fasten your skirt," but every time I had almost got the button done up, she'd roar with laughter again and fall back down on the bed.

Mum and I always enjoyed silly, "rear end" humour. One fresh spring day on one of her visits out west, we were strolling down a lane beside the sea on Mayne Island. Many of the houses on the Gulf Islands are summer getaways, and the residents love to name them. In front of almost every cottage or driveway is a carved piece of driftwood bearing the name of the residence and the owners' names: WOODPECKER HIDE-A-WAY—THE WILSONS; DROP ANCHOR—CAROL AND BUTCH BIRD; MARINE MEADOWS—THE BLACKS. When we passed a cottage with a sign carved in the shape of a lighthouse that read, WINDY SHORES—THE BUTTS, Mum and I convulsed in laughter, so much so that we tumbled into the ditch.

Along with her Suttles & Seawinds skirt, Mum wore a crisp white blouse from L.L. Bean that Heather and Anne had given her and her Mexican glass beads. She combed her hair and put on her llama hat, and then we got into the Probe and drove down to Gallery 78, which is in a massive old house with turrets, stained glass, a carved banister, and wooden floors. It was late afternoon, and golden elm leaves were falling in a light breeze. Germaine sat Mum down on an elegant velvet settee next to Inge and gave them both a glass of white wine.

Mum and I had agreed that the money the exhibit raised would go to five charities: the Fredericton hospice, the SPCA, the city's homeless shelter, Transition House, and the local art school in Saint Andrews where Mum had taught. After Dad died, we discovered that he had left a hefty sum to several homeless shelters in his will. I had never heard him mention homeless people, but I think he had never forgotten the severe poverty his family experienced when they arrived in Toronto and had to eat restaurant scraps and sleep in boxes. He loved Canada and was very thankful for his successes here, and he especially loved New Brunswick.

The gallery was packed. It seemed as if half the town had turned out for the show, even the chief of police, who was a woman with a great sense of humour. At the end, just for fun, we auctioned off five items I had saved when Mum left the house: Dad's tomato seeds, which he called "Bruno's Best"; his walking stick; his salmon flies; his cookbooks; and, the best item of all, the decal for his disability parking permit, which didn't expire until 2017. "Bruno stole that from Ernie, his brother in Hamilton," Mum whispered to me. The decal went for a good price, and I threw in Dad's old car air freshener as a bonus. The evening was great fun, and Mum reconnected with all her old Fredericton friends. Germaine sold almost everything, and in the end we made thousands of dollars for the charities.

After the grand event, Mum and I trudged (or staggered or lumbered; neither of us ever walked gracefully) across the street to the Beaverbrook Hotel for a late dinner. We loved the place. The dining room was dated, with a worn, dark-red carpet and yellowed walls covered in velvet paintings of river scenes, but the service was good, with white linen tablecloths and napkins, butter in a dish, and a nice basket of bread delivered before the meal. Both of us ordered fish chowder and salad. "I like the veterans' home," Mum said, "but this place is so civilized."

Sometimes Mum and I went through the old photograph albums she'd brought with her when she left her house on Kensington Court. That gave us pleasure on stormy afternoons during my visits. Outside, leaves would be blowing along the dark streets under a low, cold sky. Inside, Mum and I were happily reminiscing in her warm room, looking at pictures, and listening to Elgar. A tea trolley came by every day at three o'clock, handing out snacks, muffins, and other refreshments.

"And how are my darlin's today?" asked one jovial nurse who was pushing the trolley.

When she pushed on to the next room, Mum whispered, "How dare she call us darlin's! Is she the one who chews gum? There's one nurse who chews gum who is too rough with me."

I kept my eyes open after Mum said that, observing every nurse carefully, but I never saw any rough treatment.

One afternoon I came across a blue cloth-bound book in Mum's basket of papers and photographs. "Oh, that's that book of poems Bill Glassco gave me," Mum said as I handed it to her. Mum's old friend Bill was a theatre director who had founded the Tarragon Theatre in Toronto. Mum opened the book and showed me what he had written on the first page:

Poems about flowers,
and Time,
and Love,
and you-name-it;
poems about Life.
To Molly, with love from Bill

Under that, in her shaky handwriting, Mum had added, "And Bill, I'm passing this treasure on to Anny."

Mum had been planning to give me the book at some point, she said, and now seemed the perfect time. She and I loved to look through old photos and clippings and belongings, reviewing the past happily. During those moments, we both became very generous, especially after a vermouth or two. Gran had had that trait as well. "You like it? Take it," she'd say to a visitor who admired an antique Chinese jade candle holder she'd taken from Harold's house when she moved to Galiano. So it was this spontaneity that led me to take possession of the treasured poetry book Bill Glassco had given Mum.

The collection contained poems by Canadians like Alden Nowlan, P.K. Page, and Al Purdy, but also poetry by Yeats and many others, including "The Elephant Is Slow to Mate" by D.H. Lawrence. Mum and I leafed through them with delight. I read aloud an excerpt from "A Coney Island of the Mind 29," by the American poet Lawrence Ferlinghetti: "And there they all are struggling toward each other or after each other like those marble maidens on that Grecian Urn or on any market street . . ."

Mum and I often discussed poetry. Before I die, I really would like to understand how the images, metaphors, and meanings in poetry work. Oftentimes it looks so simple, but it's not. I have tried on three occasions to write a poem, and these were the topics: the shape of men's legs (something I had noticed as they jogged past me every morning when I walked Archie along the sea wall in Victoria—some legs were so pudgy, and others so sinewy); Mr. Darcy meets Mel Brooks (that was Mum's idea—what two of her favourite men might say if they met each other); and bodily fluids. Patsy and I had once visited the Museum of Modern Art in New York to see an exhibit titled *Bodily Fluids*. It was revolting—two rows of large silver jugs labelled pus, snot, spit, sweat, and so on. I said to Patsy over mimosas in the gallery café afterwards, "I think that was disgusting." She said, "What's the matter, are you ashamed of the human body?" and I said, "Yes, Patsy, I am, especially of the liquids!" I started to write a poem about how I would never be able to swim in public pools or take saunas after seeing that exhibit, but halfway through I realized I didn't care that much after all.

I would give Mum the news from Victoria on every visit, how my raised beds in the backyard were doing, and what Archie and I had seen on our beach roams, and what kinds of garbage I had encountered on my rounds—when I was at home, I picked up a bag of street or beach trash almost every day. Once a month for a treat, I told her, I'd started walking down to the Empress Hotel on Victoria's Inner Harbour for a special cocktail made with basil and mint. "Oh, the Empress," Mum chuckled. "I used to go there with Mum to listen to Billy Tickle and his trio!" Mum and I both got a kick out of quirky word combinations and tongue twisters. She often recited a favourite from her childhood—"One smart fellow, he felt smart, two smart fellows, they both felt smart, three smart fellows, they all felt smart." Sometimes Mum would say, "Oh, I long for the west and to go home," but I felt sure that her heart had adapted to love New Brunswick and her dear friends there. I had offered many times to "abduct" her and take her back to Victoria, but she always refused.

At some point, I got the idea of purchasing Dad's big Toyota Venza from his estate and driving it home to Victoria. Mum and Dad and I had driven from Fredericton to Vancouver and back in the 1960s, when I was about eight, in Dad's green Buick. I had befriended a little tabby cat while we were visiting Gran on Galiano Island, and Mum and Dad decided I could bring him home. We named him Pierre, after Pierre Trudeau. I remember being in Banff with Pierre. For some reason I had put him on a long elastic rope, and we were leaning over a balcony, looking at the magnificent views of the mountains, when Pierre leaped off the railing—he bounced up and down like a yoyo! Somebody reached down and retrieved him. In Saskatchewan, under the hot prairie sun, we were pulled over by a siren. Dad stayed calm and rolled down his window as the police officer approached our car. The policeman said, "I see you're from New Brunswick." "Yes, we are," said Dad. "Well, I'm from Cape Tormentine," said the officer, "and I was just wondering if you could say hello to my folks when you get back." Mum and Dad laughed about that for years.

I planned to leave Fredericton in the Venza at the crack of dawn, so as to arrive in Quebec City by lunch. My friend Mikki was flying out from Victoria to meet me there. I was nervous, of course, about crashing the car, getting a flat tire, or missing the turn to the bridge that spanned the mighty St. Lawrence and not being able to speak French to ask for help. However, I was determined to go. Because I wanted to leave so early, I thought it best if I stayed up the street from the veterans' home at the Fredericton Inn the night before. Mum understood. I told her I'd call as soon as I arrived at the Hotel Frontenac in Quebec City, but she said, "No, call me from Winnipeg."

After dinner in the facility's dining room (the kitchen staff always set up a table for us in a corner, so we could eat together in private and enjoy our Jost wine), I folded up the quilt the nurses had given me for the cot and pulled off the sheets. I helped Mum into her nightie and turned on her radio. To her delight, CBC was running a repeat of a Michael Enright program.

I planned to return in a couple of months. "Late summer," I said, "and then we'll go to the Digby Pines."

Mum sighed. "Oh, the Digby Pines. What a wonderful thing to look forward to."

So off I went, into the night, into the Venza and up a couple of blocks to the Fredericton Inn. I had a martini in the dark bar and then a hot bath in my room. I wrote a little in my diary at the Arborite desk and then studied my route—up to the Quebec border through Grand Falls, then Edmundston—before dozing off.

I woke at three o'clock and decided to leave then—I felt as if I were on a great adventure. Outside, I could see my breath, along with every star in the sky. I set off down the empty highway and felt a surge of the most wonderful freedom and calmness, independent power of a certain kind.

Mikki and I enjoyed the trip immensely, and it made me love Canada more than I ever had thought possible. For the first time in ages, Mum and Dad were not the main thing on my mind; Dad was gone, and Mum was happily dozing in a home for tired veterans. Getting to know my great, vast country was my new security—if I couldn't have my parents, I would embrace Canada instead. I think Mum and Dad would have been proud to know how I felt. They both loved Canada so much. I heard Dad yell at a student at the university on the issue once. The student was complaining, "Nothing ever happens in Canada," and Dad shouted, "Well, that's the beauty of the place, for Christ's sake!"

I phoned Mum from Winnipeg as promised, but she couldn't talk for long. She'd been afflicted with a horrendous cough and was resting. "I'm fine. It's just my damn old throat. I can't swallow very well, so the nurses are making me milkshakes." Mum never wanted anyone to worry.

When Mikki and I drove through Swift Current, Saskatchewan, I thought of my friend Lorna Crozier, who grew up there. When I had Glamorgan Farm, Lorna and her husband, Patrick Lane, would come for dinner and we'd wander around the farm gardens at dusk. Lorna would help me lock up the animals for the night—the hens would be on their perches, eyes closed and making a low cackling sound, the pigs would be deep in their hay beds, and the horses would be hanging their necks to sleep under the Garry oaks in the meadow. Lorna and Patrick always volunteered to do readings in my huge barn loft for charity events. The three of us remained good friends after I moved into town from North Saanich, where they still live. Funny about friends. I never see them, but I still consider them close. We pass in the night, truly—one evening Patrick was doing a poetry reading downtown, and a block away I was buying underwear at The Bay.

Mum loved to get together with Lorna and Patrick when she visited me out west. "They speak Canadian," she would always say. Lorna wrote a poem titled "In Moonlight"; it's not long, but it's beautiful, and I read it to Mum on one of her visits. Our favourite line was, "*The garden going on/without us.*" Mum and I both treasured that thought, in different ways. It makes me feel good that even after I die, life will go on, all life, that maybe my ashes will nourish a honeysuckle bush, or my spirit will settle in a wild currant shrub in a woodland, but Mum didn't like the thought of endings—they made her downcast. She wasn't at ease with death. I don't think she ever wanted to die—she wanted to be part of the garden forever. Her paintings were always bursting with life and energy.

Finally, Mikki and I reached Vancouver. The ferry trip from Vancouver to Victoria is very beautiful; people from all over the world come to see our breathtaking ocean landscapes. Sometimes you pass a pod of orca whales or see bald eagles carrying food to their young in huge stick nests up on the bluffs. There's a rocky area with shallow water between Mayne and Galiano Islands where sea lions collect to sunbathe and bark. A huge Russian ship ran aground on that rock when I was young and staying with Gran one summer; her house was on the grassy slope just up the road.

I'd spent most summers as a kid on Galiano Island with Gran. The trolls always accompanied me; I'd play with them all day outdoors in Gran's garden, in the small tent she set up for me. There was one awful day when the trolls almost drowned. Gran's house was on a beautiful sandstone shelf that sloped gently into the sea, and when the tide went out, it left many warm little tidal pools that were full of life. I was in heaven playing there. One afternoon the trolls were swimming in a tidal pool, wearing bathing caps I had made for them by cutting up old balloons, when a BC ferry passed by and created a turbulent wave that swept the trolls out to sea. I screamed in horror. Mum was there at the time, smoking and sunning herself with a friend. They came running down, leaped into the cold, green sea, and rescued all the trolls. I was hysterical—I did mouth-to-mouth on each troll in the moss up on the foreshore, bringing them back to life. I remember the horror so well. It was the worst day of my life to that point, and I'd say it still is.

Beyond Gran's place there was a ridge of arbutus trees, and it was from that ridge that Mum threw Gran's ashes into the sea. Mum often told the story of coming out from the east to pick up Gran's ashes from the funeral home on nearby Salt Spring Island. Mum was given the ashes in a large bag, which she took with her on the ferry to Galiano. She hiked up to the arbutus glade on the ridge and threw the contents of the bag over the cliff, but instead of ashes, Gran's blue smock and other clothing tumbled down the rocks into the water. Mum had been given the bag containing Gran's clothing by mistake. Mum said it was sadder than throwing Gran's ashes, to see her mum's Simpsons-Sears smock blown by the wind into the churning sea.

IT WAS FUNNY about Dad's Venza—Mikki and I drove it all the way across Canada without incident, but as we approached our driveway in Victoria, the monster car felt too cumbersome to park. We had to reverse and turn and go forward and reverse a few more times to get it in the narrow driveway. After that, we could barely open the doors, because the driveway was lined with blooming red and purple poppies.

We were happy to be home. The cats appeared from their attic hiding places and rubbed up against our luggage. A neighbour had fed them for us while we were gone. Pip was chirping in his cage, there was a stack of mail to open, the garden had grown out of control, and the lawn needed mowing.

I called Mum, and she answered in a feeble voice. "I'm a sick old lady," she said. My heart sank. But I cheered her up and said I would return soon. I told her that Dad's car was too big for our driveway and that I was going to trade it in for a smaller vehicle. "Good idea," she whispered. I said goodbye, because I could tell she was tired. "They're really kind to me here," Mum said before we hung up. I thought maybe she was just having a bad day. I had noticed when I was there that Mum had days when she felt energetic and positive, and other days when she was simply exhausted.

I went back to work, teaching English at a language school downtown. After walking Archie at dawn along the beachfront, I would have breakfast and then walk to work through my neighbourhood, past Emily Carr's birthplace with its circular English garden, then beside the solid stone Legislative Buildings with their green copper domes, along the

Inner Harbour, past the Empress Hotel, and through the rose garden, where almost every afternoon there was a wedding.

Before I entered the school, an old, red-brick building with huge windows of thick glass, I usually bought a coffee. When I carry my coffee in my travel mug across the street to work, I feel the lovely calmness of being normal, just like everyone else at that moment—or like all the normal people, anyway. My classroom is large and airy with white walls and a long windowsill I have filled with plants. My language students love *Anne of Green Gables*, and I read them First Nation stories too.

I got back to my regular weekend routines as well. I rode Valnah, the Russian horse I board at a lovely place near Victoria General hospital, and Mikki and I often took Archie for a swim at Elk/Beaver Lake, in a wooded park near town. Mum did a painting years ago of the crowded Elk Lake beach on a summer day—the painting is now part of the permanent collection of the Charlottetown Art Gallery.

In preparation for selling the Venza, I vacuumed the seats, polished the dash, and shook out the mats. When I opened the compartment between the two front seats, I found a treasure: a sketchbook of Dad's, full of drawings, recipes, cartoons, salmon-smokehouse plans and measurements, and other notes. Everything was done in pencil in Dad's impeccably neat block printing. He'd drawn the details of various fly-fishing knots, in particular the turle knot. His winter bird-food recipe—one part peanut butter, two parts birdseed, five parts cornmeal, one part suet melted, then cooled—was accompanied by a sketch of the bird feeder he had designed to hang from a tree and keep the squirrels away. There were numerous lovely sketches of river scenes and fishing camps. He had titled one scene *The Bass Hole* and noted on another, regarding a camp he had visited, "Poor fishing and flies galore." There was a building design for something called Adam's Snore Shack. Along with sketches of his fishing pals in their hip waders, wielding nets and rods, there was an exquisite drawing of a poor little mouse in a trap. There was even a sketch of Ottawa's Parliament Buildings. Dad must have done it when he went to receive his Order of Canada—he was terrified of flying, but he couldn't resist going to get his little white pin from the Governor General at the time, the attractive and intelligent Michaëlle Jean. There were comments on a card game—"Dumb game," he had written, "takes too many matches"—and a recipe for wallpaper paste. A page entitled "Bruno's Cold Smoked Salmon Fillets" gave instructions for salting, curing, rinsing, drying ("best done on a windy day"), and finally smoking. I also found a little sketch Dad had done of the river just in front of his camp, the place Mum and I would cool our feet and slap away mosquitoes while sipping our vermouth. I tucked Dad's notebook away in a safe place, slipping it into the box where I kept my thirty trolls, a lock of hair from my first horse, and Gran's chipped enamel cream skimmer.

I continued to visit Mum regularly, catching up on National Film Board shorts, documentaries, and animations on my flights across the country. We made the odd day trip from Fredericton when she was feeling well enough. In Saint Andrews, we had our usual lobster soup and then sat on the rocky beach in front of the Gleason Arms, where Mum found a pair of false teeth. We drove around the town, admiring its old homes and churches; one of the churches, a sign said, was closing down because its congregation had dwindled to three people. William Cornelius Van Horne, the wealthy president of the Canadian Pacific who saw the railway built to completion, had a summer estate on Ministers Island, just off Saint Andrews' main street. The place is being restored by volunteers, and when the tide is out, you can walk across the rocks to the island.

Van Horne's main home was in a wealthy part of Montreal, and it was there he met the Canadian painter James Wilson Morrice. Van Horne bought one of Morrice's first oil paintings, a large, dark landscape of a grove of trees on a hill in France. When the painting ended up years later in a gallery in Victoria, I bought it; nobody else in Canada seemed to want it. It is rather crude, an early work, not one of the exquisite beach or street scenes Morrice became famous for, but I think the big painting is historic. Perhaps one day someone will organize an exhibition that showcases all of Morrice's work, including that early piece with its ornate golden frame.

CHAPTER TEN

IT WAS LATE FEBRUARY IN 2014, just a few days before Mum's ninety-fourth birthday, and I'd come back to Fredericton to help her celebrate. The sun was shining, icicles dripped, and gritty water flowed along the sidewalks as the snowdrifts shrank. The parking lot at the Veterans Health Unit had become bare pavement, so I bundled Mum up in her winter coat, scarf, and Cowichan mitts and took her out in her wheelchair to get some fresh air.

The air was crisp and clean as we made our way around the perimeter of the parking lot. Back indoors, I settled Mum on the blue velour couch in the lounge and propped her up with four pillows—she coughed less when she sat up straight—then covered her with Judy's purple quilt. Susan, a sweet woman who worked in the kitchen, made Mum banana milkshakes every evening, along with cream soups and puddings, and she would bring them to the lounge on a tray. Mum thought back to the first time she'd had a milkshake. "Lawrence took me to Stanley Park," she told me, referring to her half-brother, "and for a shin plaster [a bill worth twenty-five cents], he bought me a vanilla milkshake at English Bay." I poured a glass of wine for myself, and Mum moved in and out of a gentle sleep. Everything seemed right with the world at that moment.

The devoted night nurses often stopped to chat with Mum on their rounds. Claire was small, slim, and perpetually busy, always passing briskly with a load of clean towels or pushing some big, purple, plastic machine down the hall. Mum loved Claire—she was so sweet and gentle and seemed so sensible (something that I find a great comfort in a nurse). Kathy always smelled beautiful, an exotic combination of herbal medicines and soap. She wore white uniforms, like a storybook nurse, and had a wonderful, open, smiling face. I would see her in the hall, mixing drugs and putting drops and pills into small plastic cups for each resident. Gail was very calm and down-to-earth. Claire, Kathy, and Gail seemed to Mum and me exactly what nurses should be—what good people should be, for that matter—driven not by ego but by compassion and kindness.

The Olympics were coming to an end, and we watched the closing ceremonies on the television in the lounge. The Russian Children's Choir sang the wonderful Russian national anthem, which brought Mum and me to tears. We agreed again that Russians have such soul, despite Putin. They are a rough people, but with deep feeling, and that juxtaposition makes them fascinating.

Sometimes I needed a break from the vets. I craved fresh air and the chance to move, so I embarked on various afternoon outings when Mum was asleep. If I turned to the right when I got outside, I'd pass the bleak hospital, head through a bare industrial area, and walk downhill through the university gates. The hospital was an ugly box, which was a shame; hospitals above all kinds of architecture should be pleasing—stimulating but restful. The newly renovated hospital in Victoria is stunning that way, with large, naturally lit spaces, tumbling water, and cultural icons such as totem poles and public art. Best of all, a spacious patio of lavender beds incorporates the rock of the hill, featuring graceful trees and grasses and private seating areas. A small chapel is tucked among the gardens, and the hospital has a renovated, old-fashioned surgical room. It's a delight, a calming and beautiful setting.

The University of New Brunswick is on a massive, sprawling slope, providing views of the rambling Saint John River, the old iron railway bridge, and the copper steeple of the cathedral. The stroll down through the campus is a lovely walk, especially toward the bottom, where towering elms and maples line the pathways. Dad did a painting of the university gates that later appeared on a Canadian stamp. Over the years, he also did many portraits of professors and other notable people associated with the university. Mum painted many university scenes as well, especially sports teams and convocations. The university became a large part of their lives when we moved to New Brunswick in the early 1960s.

At the bottom of the university, across the railway tracks, there's a beautiful, winding path that leads to downtown. In warmer months, the trail is lined with wildflowers and shrubs—daisies, tansy, chokecherry, clover, and buttercups. It's paved now, but I can still remember the smell of mud and vegetation from the summers when Mum and I walked along the trail to the Saturday market.

The trail leading from the university gates also veers left, toward Regent Street, passing the rink that used to be brick and turquoise and the park where I came third in high jumping in a junior high school track meet. Sometimes, before going back to the veterans' facility I'd stop at the liquor store in the restored train station. The nurses were generous in sharing their kitchen, so I'd chill Mum's wineglasses in their freezer and put the pickled onions I bought for my martinis in the fridge. I had set up a little bar in Mum's room by the cool window, and it was delightful to invite her visitors to have a drink. "A lemon twist? Olives?" I'd ask them once they were settled in the overstuffed yellow chair Mum had brought with her from the house.

Another of my afternoon outings was to walk farther up the hill and across the highway to a mall. That was more amusing than it sounds. The mall had a bookstore and a coffee shop where I'd sit and write and drink espressos and eat organic blueberry squares. But the best part about that outing was the Fredericton Inn, a big brick motel with dated yellow stucco arches adorning each level of windows. The inn's cozy, dim lounge became my sanctuary; I'd sit in the corner in a beige polyester tub chair with a glass of wine and think about nothing. Sometimes I made lists of the things I had to do when I got home to Victoria—call the foot nurse to cut my nails, refill the beer in my greenhouse containers to get rid of the slugs, have my friend Joan over for a drink. Joan owned a three-legged rescue dog from Kuwait named Hazel, who was Archie's best friend.

One evening I was relaxing in the corner of the Fredericton Inn's lounge after a big day. Mum and I had been outside in the sunshine. Mum had eaten a whole bowl of cream of broccoli soup, and I'd read a chapter of Catherine the Great's biography to her, the part when Catherine, then named Sophia, travels from Germany to Saint Petersburg in the winter, over frozen, rutted ground, wrapped in furs, to meet the Empress Elizabeth. After that we'd had visits from Mum's dear old friend Cora, a true soulmate, and from a Legion lady who left a Kit Kat bar on Mum's bed.

That evening there was a small party of older people gathered around the bar in the inn. A man with a big belly and a cowboy hat was drinking a beer. Another man, pink-cheeked, in big beige shorts that revealed pale, hairy calves, was trying to catch nuts in his mouth. A couple of women were eating pretzels with their rum and Cokes, and an energetic woman with dyed red hair and wearing a red suit was running around selling tickets for a draw. A tall, weathered woman in snug jeans, her hair cropped like a brush cut, strutted over to my peaceful corner with her thumbs in her belt loops. "Mind if I join you?" she asked. She sat down, interrupting thoughts I wasn't really having, and took a big gulp of her frothy pink cocktail. "How long have you been with OFFSC?" she inquired.

"Pardon?" I said. It turned out that OFFSC stood for Over Forties Fredericton Social Club, and that they met once a week for drinks at the Fredericton Inn.

"We call ourselves 'over forty,' but in truth, we're all over sixty," said the woman, rising and straightening her jeans over her sinewy thighs.

The night nurses let me back into the veterans' unit. The halls were silent, and the staff were doing paperwork in their fluorescently lit office. The residents were asleep except for one nice fellow roaming the halls with his walker.

"I just can't sleep much," he confided as we walked together past the dining area. It was all set for breakfast, with blue cloth bibs folded neatly at each place. "Your mother talks about the west often," he said. "I think she wants to go there."

"Well," I said, "I've tried to abduct her many times."

He chuckled. Mum was sleeping peacefully when I got back to her room.

On the final day of my visit, Mum turned ninety-four. She was frail, but she rose to the occasion. I got her dressed in a clean white blouse and a lovely cotton sweater that Heather and Anne had given her. Mum combed her own hair, and I held her up by the sink so she could brush her teeth. I had become adept at working with Mum and holding her from behind, with my arms under hers. My main problem was figuring out the brakes on her wheelchair. I wheeled her down the hall for our morning stroll, and when we passed the dining area, the kitchen staff all came out from the hot kitchen in their hairnets and baggy cotton pants to gather around her chair and sing "Happy Birthday." Mum smiled and nodded and shed a few tears.

Flowers and cards arrived all morning, but Mum was tired and lay back down under Judy's quilt. She'd been coughing since five o'clock (as she said, "It's the excitement of the day!") and nurse Gail gave her something called a "butterfly" to calm her, which worked.

I said, as I leaned over her bed, "Now you get strong for our next road trip to Shediac in the spring," and Mum said, "I will—I'll beat this." Her eyes closed, and she drifted off peacefully.

Mary Blatherwick picked me up at the hospital, and we had a glass of wine at the Beaverbrook as a calming transition between the veterans' facility and my long flight home across Canada.

I felt weary by the time I boarded the small plane that would take me to Toronto, too tired to read about Catherine the Great's exploits. As we climbed above the cold, green forests and lakes of New Brunswick, all I felt like doing was eating pretzels and thumbing through *enRoute* magazine. Maybe it's just me, but I take a rather disgusted view of humans regarding the trivial information we seem so desperate to find and communicate. Do we really want to know *everything*? I thought as I read an article on how to pack for your pet on vacation (hint: plastic dishes and air-sickness tablets) and then one on what to do with your old high school trophies (cut them off and use them as wine stoppers). I ordered a vodka and tonic from the flight attendant. She didn't have any lemon, but the drink cooled me off. I chewed on the ice as I read yet another article, this time on the top ten behavioural addictions. Ice chewing was one of them!

The plane rose into a blanket of dome- and cone-shaped cloud formations, bathed in a warm rose glow from the setting sun, with the ice-blue sky high above. It was like flying through a petri dish full of flourishing bacteria, beautiful little fungal growths and floating microbes all washed with a milky pink.

The next article I read was on the three best places in the world to order a hot chocolate: Chicago, Calgary, and Brighton. I'd taken the train to Brighton when I was about sixteen—my first trip alone away from home. I'd gone to England to visit my uncle Abby, and while I was there I bought Mum a little silver ring that she wore constantly. Just the year before, she'd woken up one day and couldn't find it. "I've become so thin," she said, "that the ring must have fallen off my finger." We never did find it.

England always seemed like a toy land to me, with its small scale, red-enameled post boxes, peppermint sticks, and striped deck chairs on the beaches by the seashore. In London, when Mum and Dad were teaching art and travelling, we had a small flat in Cleaver Square. Every afternoon, the ice cream cart would come by. The bell would ring, and Dad would come out and buy me a Creamsicle or a Wigwam. I spent most of my time washing and dressing the two stone lions that stood at the foot of our steps. I would talk to them in a low whisper for hours as I tied scarves and rain hats onto their cool, grey heads. Mum walked me to school every morning, and we'd often pass a tiny lady—in those days we would refer to her as a midget—who carried a green umbrella and wore a brown coat that hung on her little body in a perfect oval shape.

Mum's life had been so rich and full, and it seemed strange to me that now the world was saturated with such useless information as where to buy the best hot chocolate. That's what I was thinking as we landed in Toronto, the CN Tower visible in the haze in the distance. Every time I saw it, I thought of Rick Mercer and Jann Arden hanging off the top ledge in red survival suits and helmets on one episode of Rick's television show.

Mum died three days later, on February 29. It didn't come as a shock, because lovely nurse Kathy (road sister name "Fluffy") had called me every day to tell me that Mum was sleeping more and more deeply. "Nice even, slow breaths," she said, which reminded me of what we were supposed to achieve in yoga class. When Kathy called to say the time was very near, late on a Friday night, I was sitting in a comfy chair with a martini, listening to the pounding rain outside, with Catherine the Great on one knee and my large, furry, drooling cat Sophie on the other.

When I received the final call two hours later, I didn't feel like an orphan, as I'd expected. Perhaps that was just an old cliché. I had always felt slightly like an orphan anyway, or at least very much alone. As Mum's favourite poet, Stevie Smith, put it, "I was much too far out all my life . . ."

Mum and Dad were part of a bigger world than their family. For their art to be honest and free and worthwhile, they had to be open to more than just being paternal or maternal. Children of artists and creative thinkers must accept this. We share our parents with the messages they create for the rest of the world. Mum and I had bonded tightly, but not so much as mother and daughter, and not as the cliché of "best friends," either. We were more like two people who shared a similar sense of humour and a compassion for the world, a deep caring. And we had such fun together on our road trips.

I'm not very maternal myself, except with my animals. Mum had said several times throughout her life that she hoped I would have a dozen children. Then she'd correct herself: "Well, at least one." And once she said the strangest thing, that having a child was the most creative thing a woman could do. But I don't think she really believed it. And I had never had the urge to have children, Mum knew. We always laughed when one of us used the word "urge." It reminded us of naughtiness or bodily functions.

Mum always said that Dad was afraid of germs—"He's so clean," she'd whisper to me sometimes—and she also thought he was petrified of dying. But I am sure that at the end of Dad's life, he was calm and contented—I saw it when I was with him. In Mum's final days, I never knew if she really thought she had something minor or if she knew she was dying and didn't want to upset me, in case I had one of my nervous spells. That is a mystery that will never be solved.

AFTER MUM'S DEATH, I found great comfort in strolling the beaches in the winter drizzle. I'd walk in the early dawn with Archie to Clover Point and watch the sun rise. But sometimes I'd see the oystercatchers and I'd think to myself, I must describe this to Mum, and then I'd realize she wasn't there to tell, and I had no desire to tell anyone else.

Mum had loved to hear descriptions of the activity, weather, and scenery in Victoria: the canopy of cherry blossoms on a neighbouring street; the first dandelion of the year in the meadow along Dallas Road; the huge blue heron nests made of sticks high in the trees in Beacon Hill Park; the tidal pools on the beach; or my garden with its enormous kale that I ate all winter. I'd relay my observations on the Victoria Day parade to her—the winning floats one year were from the Monarchist League (a lot of purple and gold velvet) and the Infertility Clinic. The White Eagle Polish Hall's float was great too. Simple, everyday things made us chuckle—simplicity means so much when you grow old.

Mum also loved to hear about Archie. She always asked, "How are Archie and the pussycats?" "Archie and I went to the beach," I'd report, "and he had a great romp with his best friend, Hazel. She can outrun him on a straight stretch with her three legs, but the corners give her trouble," or "Archie has taken to eating kelp, and it gives him the runs," or "There was a mother otter with four babies out on the rocks. Archie clambered out to investigate and the mother became upset and threatened him. Archie made a speedy retreat, back to the pebbled beach."

There were other topics I had learned to avoid. I could tell that Mum was irked and irritated, even on the other end of the telephone five thousand miles away, if I mentioned my horse, anything *inside* my house, my work teaching English, my writing, or a cultural event I had attended, so I stuck to the topics she was interested in. I love having pedicures (my bunion often aches unbearably), but that was another "off" topic, I think due to its being a costly luxury. But I had to tell Mum once what my pedicurist had said—it was so funny. There was a Salvador Dali exhibit in Vancouver that I had seen; it was quite amusing, featuring Dali's *Lips Sofa* and so on. As the pedicurist was massaging my poor, calloused feet, I asked her, "Oh, have you seen Dali in Vancouver?" and she answered, "No, we're not Buddhists anymore." She thought I was referring to the Dalai Lama! Mum and I just cracked up.

Sometimes the sunrise on Dallas Road is overwhelming in its beauty. If Mum were still here, I could tell her about the pearly apricot dawn light rising in the haze over the steel-grey sea, and the smoky-blue herringbone pattern hovering above the glow. Actually, I'm not sure I would use the words "pearly" or "apricot" or "steel-grey" or "smoky-blue"—Mum knew colours better than I do, and she might think my choice of words a bit pretentious or imprecise. I recall her telling me once about a thunderstorm over Manitoba on a flight to Fredericton. "The pilot asked us to fasten our belts," she said, "and implied we were in grave danger. You could have heard a pin drop. Everyone was silent as the plane descended through an ominous charcoal and saffron sky."

I have had small moments of rebellion too. A few months after Mum died, I bought a bouquet of yellow gladioli at a grocery store on my way to work. I put them on my desk, and everyone admired them. On my way home, I bought two more bouquets for the house. I said to myself, "Sorry, Mum, but I like these flowers." And when I put them in a vase in the living room, the sky didn't fall in. Now I buy glads regularly, and I often take them to friends' houses when I'm invited for dinner.

I never asked Dad if he liked glads. He often picked small bouquets from his garden—sweet lily of the valley or a delicate bunch combining parsley, an apple blossom, and a violet. He spent one summer doing watercolours of flowers, which he made into cards. After he died, I sent the cards to people he loved, including his doctor. She got the forget-me-nots.

I'd love to tell Mum now about the glorious broom and gorse bushes that cling to the cliffs on Dallas Road and give off the slight smell of coconut as Archie and I walk through the cold, salty morning air. Above the bluffs, the meadows are covered in camas flowers, and the air is filled with the clean scent of new leaves on the Indian plum. The grassy slope of Beacon Hill Park is a mass of daffodils nodding in the breeze.

In our back garden, behind the jasmine that will flower any day, my arugula has reached the ceiling of the greenhouse, the spinach is up to my waist, and the mustard leaves are the size of my hands. The determined mint has pushed up through the beds and is falling over the ledges. Mum would appreciate this abundance, these wonders of nature. She understood the thrill of seeing new growth bursting forth, and she captured that life force in her art.

There was one other topic Mum was keen to hear about, and that was the Gulf Islands. I'd describe the grand bonfires I made at our property on Mayne Island, how the wild quince shrub needed a good pruning, or that I'd seen the first hummingbird of the year flitting among the blackberries. Not long after she died, I went over to Mayne for a weekend to clean up the garden and rake the branches that had blown down in the winter storms. I lit a big fire and worked until dusk, as the sun sank slowly behind the giant cedar trees. I stirred the last of the embers, breathing in the wonderful combination of smells: woodsmoke, damp cedar boughs, and the ocean that lapped on the sandstone shores across the road.

This was the west coast Mum had loved so much: the carpet of snowdrops under a beech grove along Dallas Road; a bright crescent moon in the navy sky above Beacon Hill Park, with Venus floating nearby; the turbulent, green sea crashing onto the black rocks; the seagulls sitting atop the James Bay chimneys; the two crows building their nest in the hawthorn tree outside my living room window. Mum and Dad used to feed two crows in their garden. One year the pair had four youngsters, and one of them was pure white. Mum told me that the parents cared for their white offspring for years, even when it became an adult—the white crow never left home.

The crows building their nest in my hawthorn dive-bomb Archie and me when their babies hatch. I forgive them—their babies are everything to them, and protecting them is what the crows are born to do. I sometimes bring them some of the soft hair my horse sheds for their nests, leaving it in the grass among the bluebells beneath the tree.

Mum's ashes were spread on both coasts. They came in a luxurious blue velvet bag, along with a stack of documents—how strange it is that after we die, we are subjected to so much paperwork. From a high cliff on Galiano Island, I tossed her into the wind, aiming for the churning, green current below. The wind was blustery, though, and most of her came to rest in a scraggly, old arbutus tree.

On a damp, raw April day at low tide, I scrambled down the rocks to the small beach in front of the Gleason Arms in Saint Andrews, where Mum had spent some of her happiest times. I spilled her into a tidal pool, and there she mingled with an array of busy sea life—snails and barnacles and seaweeds in ochre and vermilion—until a wave carried her out into the turbulent Atlantic surf.

MOLLY LAMB BOBAK was born in Burnaby, British Columbia, in 1920. She studied art under Jack Shadbolt at the Vancouver School of Art and joined the Canadian army in 1942, becoming the only female uniformed war artist in 1945.

BRUNO BOBAK was born in Wawelowka, Poland, in 1923. He trained as an artist in Toronto, Ontario, and went on to become one of Canada's youngest war artists, commissioned in 1944.

After the war ended, Molly and Bruno married. They painted and exhibited throughout Europe, and they had two children. In 1960, they moved to Fredericton, New Brunswick, where Bruno was appointed artist in residence at the university. From 1962 until his retirement in 1987, Bruno was director of the University of New Brunswick Art Centre.

Fredericton, New Brunswick, became Molly and Bruno's permanent home, and they painted and exhibited their art throughout Canada for many years. Both received the Order of Canada for their contributions to the country. Molly made regular visits to the west coast; Bruno's passion was fly-fishing on the Miramichi River and smoking salmon at his beloved camp.

Bruno died in 2013 at the age of eighty-nine; Molly died a year later, at ninety-four.

ACKNOWLEDGMENTS

I'd like to thank my loyal publishers, Pat Touchie and Taryn Boyd at TouchWood Editions, for their support and for giving me the freedom to write my thoughts. Huge gratitude to my brilliant editor, Barbara Pulling, whom I completely trust and who has seen numerous "over the top" paragraphs, which she elegantly put a long pencil mark through.

Also, an enormous thank-you to my partner, Mikki, who worked tirelessly on the technical editing and remained calm when I thought the computer had lost one hundred pages. Deep appreciation for Germaine Pataki at Gallery 78 in Fredericton for her assistance and support. Finally, I thank Anne, Heather, and Mary for extending their support and friendship to Mum and Dad, and now to me.

ANNY SCOONES was raised in Fredericton, New Brunswick, has
served as an elected city councillor, and now teaches English in
Victoria. Anny lives in the neighbourhood of James Bay in Victoria,
British Columbia.